Responses to *Untitled* (eye with comet) (c.1985) by Paul Thek

Pilot Press
London

Constellations. NYC, August 10, 1988

Pluto stayed long in Scorpio
starting its transit way before
my sun has risen, leaving
for another sign half a decade
after Thek's leaving
like a comet and its dust
we can look farther now:
the sun was in Leo
the same sun
who saw his last sigh
the art and the cry
returning for a kiss
in 77 light years
as the photo negative

E.R. De Siqueira

Four Skies for a Comet

If a mold
Had not been taken
As it fell through
The sky
Whatever was
In that fire
Or was not
In that fire changed
The color of the smoke
In the corpse of its impact
In that open space
Of false ground then
Recovered by
The sky as the sky once laid
As steady as that eye
In the painting painted
That one humid summer afternoon

*

Stars can still
Also be invisible
At night the darkness
And smoke
Will cover them
And the darkness
Can cover the smoke
I know stars
Can breathe in the dark
And I know
Their pain of difficult
Breath their pain
Is the death of
The very first born
Breathing slow dark water
As beautifully cool
As an autumn evening

*

But let's give
Grace to what's mere-
Ly fatal-
Ly star-
Ry here in our empty sky
It did little good we're
Too old now
To cry against snow
Or dirt or stars shooting out
Over these faces
I don't know what
Exactly it is
I've drawn here seems like
Some kind of a chain
Some kind of a star
Or charm
For winter nights

*

Cloud monuments
And skyward
Accidents scatter
Stars as
The first light
Hits the garden with
Reddish-brown light that shines
Brightly on nothing but half
Heard cowboys singing
Songs softly sung inside or
Sung outside laying underneath the
Dark walnut tree dusty and
Singing and staring and
Seeing straight through
Our fated future now sung
With the breaking of
This spring morning.

Ben Estes

João Motta Guedes

Interpreting one against interpretation

Susan Sontag credited Paul Thek with the title and inspiration for *Against Interpretation*, released as part of the eponymous book in 1966. And yet, here I am, decades later offering an interpretation of a work whose name offers no more than the literal content of the form. I hope the following is read in the Nietzchian sense, of there being no facts, only interpretations, read as an offering or suggestion, of what I see while looking into Thek's *Untitled (Eye with Comet)*.

Looking beyond the careful carelessness of the daubed purple, gold and blue paint, the translucent layers suggest to me that the comet came first, that this painting is about the comet and its significance in Thek's mind's eye. A comet that obstructed, consumed Thek's vision. A portent, skidding across the lens of a golden eye, as a swan might land on water. Its wake, a whisper of the path travelled etched into the sky before disintegrating into dust, exhaled away on atmospheric winds. Throughout time, around the world, ancient civilisations understood comets to be harbingers of death and destruction, wars have been waged in the wake of comets, deaths have mounted beneath their glimmer. That the comet Halley was in the sky approaching Earth in 1985 could be everything and nothing, because regardless of erratic space travellers and their prophecies of destruction, Thek was existing in a world with no future, denied passage on the planet in which he inhabited. A life cut short through societal damnation and deficiency. Whether a comet foretold the catastrophe or not, it was rippling, ripping through the world that Thek knew with no sign of slowing and no escape from the categorisation that plagued the sick. Perhaps Thek was planning his existential departure from Earth, painting into existence a celestial ark on which to escape, riding the coattails of a comet to a place better than heaven where life is not up for judgement or interpretation, but simply is.

Lucy Swan

ROCK'S PASSING

Prophetically conjured vision,
reflected premonition. Gone
but still burning bright. Retrospectively
projecting our interpretations.
Extracting meaning without you.

True meaning hidden but
we all knew you. You are also us.
Our experiences projected liberally.
Easing open cracked window to the soul.
Symbolic reconstruction of truths unknown.

In absence of you we spend our lives
scavenging seas for burnt embers;
Shards to build altars to what never was.
Focused attentiveness. substituting
for inattentiveness when it mattered most.

Our present, the present stolen from you
Glint of hindsight. Finally revealing
the spark extinguished too soon.
Lying dormant but not lost. Your spirit
a glint in the eye for eternity.

Jon Rainford

'a secret out / of what no one / wanted anyway'

The art of Paul Thek has always been, for me, fundamentally fragmentary. His work explores memory and memorial, that which has been lost, shattered, and/or destroyed. His grandest works are tombs that are now lost; his most intimate works, reliquaries for the postmodern era, for now.

*

Stanza the sea. Earth the sea, *Fishman in Excess Table* (1970–71) [...]
    If I had only known earlier that indeterminacy involves all of life I might fathom the luminous story surrounding all things monumental.
                                        — Susan Howe, *Debths*

*

The back cover for *Paul Thek: Diver, a Retrospective* — the first retrospective devoted to Thek in the United States, in 2011 — features a photograph taken of Thek's studio at 254 East Third Street by Peter Hujar; there's a cast of his hand, tinted in wax, and a face mounted on board, eyes closed and tongue sticking out.

I recently acquired a copy of the catalogue — significantly overpaying for this hopefully invaluable trove of source and secondary material — and it now sits pride of place on my shelf alongside other Whitney publications dedicated to Andy Warhol and David Wojnarowicz. A detail of the eponymous diver painting fills the front cover: he's naked, his fingers just penetrating the skin of the water.

On page 204, there's a spread from one of Thek's notebooks: an isometric drawing of a wooden cabin — "Uncle Tom's Cabin" — on fire, flames licking the empty windows and smoke spiralling into the air. On the back cover of the Wojnarowicz catalogue — *History Keeps Me Awake At Night* — there's a reproduction of one of the artist's early stencils, a house on fire; I have this tattooed onto my right thigh. The house, the cabin is on fire. What shall we do? Let us fan the flames: burn it all down; break it all apart: let's start again.

Between 1969 and 1973, Thek created four large installation works at galleries and arts festivals across Europe, including *documenta 5*. Conceived by Thek, the works were executed by a group of friends and collaborators, including Franz Deckwitz, Edwin Klein, Cindy Lubar, Peter Hujar, Ann Wilson and Robert Wilson. They are widely considered to be amongst the most significant large-scale art installation environments of the period.

All four are now lost: only photographs, notes, and ephemera have survived. An ark, a pyramid, a tomb — vessels and monuments intended to preserve, containers for collective memory. It seems contradictory yet strangely fitting that these works have been lost — like six of the seven Wonders of the Ancient World — preserved primarily instead in memory.

*

The Procession/The Artist's Co-op at the Stedelijk Museum (1969)
Pyramid/A Work in Progress at the Moderna Museet (1971-72)
Ark, Pyramid, documenta 5 (1972)
Ark, Pyramid, Easter at the Kunstmuseum Luzern (1973)

*

Wojnarowicz dedicated a work from 1988–89 to Thek; it was first exhibited at his 1989 exhibition *In the Shadow of Forward Motion*, his first solo show since the deaths of Thek and Hujar, and his own diagnosis with HIV.

Spirituality (For Paul Thek) is seven photographs arranged on museum board; a grid of three by two above a large photograph — ants crawling across a crucifix; an image that would later elsewhere court significant controversy — as wide as three of the smaller images. Ants crawl across money; a friend — Iolo Carew, a fellow busboy from the days when Wojnarowicz worked downtown at Danceteria — exhales smoke on the couch.

Wojnarowicz presented several such photographic matrices at this exhibition; two of the work form a pair, *The Weight of the Earth, Part I* (1988) and *Part II* (1988–89), which he described as "an opera that could actually have hundreds of parts instead of just two." Both contain one small watercolour painting hidden amidst fourteen gelatin silver prints: "it's the film projectors gone convulsive; the scattering of associations, sensory and physical; […] it's an opera in the form of images where each frame is a clip from films of living sounding a particular note like each word that makes up a sentence."

At the centre of *The Weight of the Earth, Part I*, a dog wears false teeth. At the centre of *The Weight of the Earth, Part II*, an ant crawls across an unblinking wooden eye.

*

> ...and I thought of the whirling dervishes of the distant mountains across the ocean and the sources of mortality and thus possibly immortality; [...] I thought of the futurists and the arrival of the machine; [...] I thought of a painting by Paul Thek made in the months before he died of Aids entitled: THE FACE OF GOD which was a greenish painting on a sheet of newspaper of a clock face; and I thought of a photograph I made of a guy named Iolo back in 1979 lying on a couch with smoke pouring out of his mouth that reminded me vaguely of spirit leaving body and how Iolo was the first person I knew with Aids way back in the early '80's when it was called G.R.I.D....
> — David Wojnarowicz, *In the Shadow of Forward Motion*

*

Wojnarowicz dedicated two works at *In the Shadow of Forward Motion* to Peter Hujar; he was at Hujar's side when he died, taking a suite of photos of his still-warm body, eyes ajar. Photographs of the photographer, dead, whose first publication was titled *Portraits In Life And Death* — they were exhibited, untitled, at the 1989 exhibition *Witnesses: Against Our Vanishing*.

Hujar himself photographed Thek repeatedly, a witness in the artist's studio — the pair, like Hujar and Wojnarowicz, were friends and lovers and collaborators in the downtown scene. They travelled together to Italy, where Hujar photographed catacombs that would later appear in *Portraits In Life And Death*, which had a foreword by Susan Sontag, whose portrait featured alongside the photographs of rotted skulls and anonymous femurs. Sontag dedicated *Against Interpretation* (1966) to Thek; "In place of a hermeneutics we need an erotics of art."

*

In Search of a Perfect Stimulant (1979–80)
An Erotics Of Art (c. 1980)
Afflict the Comfortable, Comfort the Afflicted (c. 1985)
Susan Lecturing On Neitzsche [sic] (1987)
While There Is Time (1987)

*

"The world was falling apart, anyone could see it," Thek once noted.

In 1988, Thek, like Hujar the previous year, and Wojnarowicz in 1992, died of AIDS.

In 1989, Sontag published *AIDS and its Metaphors*: "Now the generic rebuke to life and to hope is AIDS."

*

The fragment is the intervention of death into the work.
By destroying the work, it removes from it the flaw of semblance.
— Theodor W. Adorno, *Aesthetic Theory*

*

One of Thek's most startling works is part of his *Technological Reliquaries* series, commonly referred to as the *Meat Pieces* (1964–67). *Meat Piece with Warhol Brillo* Box: the title gives away this conceit, but this push and pull of expectation is crucial to Thek's piece. The upturned Brillo Box exposes not only the artifice of Warhol's artwork — that this is painted wood, not printed cardboard, an overdetermined facsimile typical of Pop Art — but something altogether more disquieting and horrific. Get up close, peer through the plexiglass, and you see the meat is beeswax, its wiry hairs carefully placed by the artist's hand.

It was, in art world terms, a relatively swift reaction; Andy Warhol first exhibited his Brillo Boxes at the Stable Gallery in New York in 1964 and Thek exhibited his intervention just a few months later, using one of the original boxes, at the same gallery.

Also in 1964, Thek was filmed by Warhol in two of his *Screen Tests* [ST337 and ST338]: short, silent, black-and-white films made between 1964 and 1966, of which 472 survive. Fellow subjects include Salvador Dalí, Marcel Duchamp, Peter Hujar, Jonas Mekas, Jack Smith, Susan Sontag.

*

    28. Paint a series of playing balls like planets, be accurate. [...]
43. Why are you here? What is a shaman? Make a piece of curative art.
    Make a piece of psychological art. What do you think has been the greatest hurt, mental and physical, that you have suffered? [...]
44. What do you think are the qualities of a life fully lived? Can you suggest a project, for yourself or for a group, or for any number,
which might deepen your sensitivity to time? What is greed? What is verbal knowledge? What does tactile mean? Can you show me an example of tactile sensitivity in your personal life?
— Paul Thek, *Teaching Notes: 4-Dimensional Design*

*

Each of the plexiglass reliquaries contains either a severed human limb or a piece of bloodless meat: largely unidentified but, in one case, carefully labelled as 'hippopotamus'. Thek was inspired by his trip to Sicily with Hujar: "I hope the work has the innocence of those Baroque Crypts in Sicily [...] It delighted me that bodies could be used to decorate a room, like flowers. We accept our thing-ness intellectually but the emotional acceptance of it can be a joy."

In Catholic teaching, relics — objects relating to saints and other divine figures — are categorised into three classes: first class relics are the most gruesome, the body part of a saint, usually a bone, sometimes blood, generally exhumed during canonisation; second class relics are the possessions of a saint, or artefacts relating to the Virgin Mary or to Christ, such as the nails or wood of the True Cross; and third class relics are objects touched by divinity, a holy site, or another relic.

Medieval pilgrims would often return with a third class relic, a piece of contact with the divine; they were far from uncommon. First class relics were stored in reliquaries: elaborate objet d'art to house and venerate the relic contained within. Relics did not survive the Reformation; reliquaries now sit in private and public collections around the world, as well as in churches and Catholic cathedrals. They pose difficult ethical questions for conservationists and curators, with new scrutiny placed on the treatment of human remains. (Here, second and third class relics are fine, their lesser divinity suddenly a blessing.) Many reliquaries have thus been opened recently, sometimes for the first time in centuries, and others x-rayed, their contents tested: some of the bones were found not to even be human.

*

Untitled(s):
(eye with comet)
(blue bunnies and red ships)
(purple fish)
(orange squiggles)
(bunnies and ovals)
(bunnies and vortex)
(z-ing)

*

Every work by Felix Gonzales-Torres is untitled, its meaning tied up in its subtitle. In many of his works — stacks of printed posters or individually wrapped sweets, the heights and weights dictated by the artists — visitors to the gallery space are invited to take one, or more, of the constitutive pieces. He rejects the maxim of the gallery — "do not touch" — and turns it on its head: "please, take this".

Several of the so-called candy spills are portraits, of the artist's farther, or of his lover, Ross Laycock, who was dying of AIDS. Take a piece of him, let it dissolve in your mouth — at once innocent and sexual, sacred and profane — a minor transubstantiation. In the gallery, at least, he will be endlessly replenished. His works endlessly disperse themselves, are fragmented, recuperated, and reiterated.

I have a couple of posters from two stack works, one of which was exhibited in Reading Gaol. They remain unfurled in a corner; I see them more as objects than as artworks or images, traces of my own past, stood still before the stack.

González-Torres died of AIDS in 1996, yet his artworks persist. Even now, they feel alive, imbued with something of the artist, if not his touch, as perhaps with a painter, then his soul; each discrete piece a contact relic for then — for now.

*

> stand to face me beloved
> and open out the grace of your eyes
> — Sappho, *fragment 138*, tr. Anne Carson

*

Untitled (eye with comet) (c.1985): between the visual and the mystical, between the actual and the esoteric. "Eye with comet"; not, "comet with eye"; nor, "eye and comet". The eye has supremacy.

Wojnarowicz's photograph of an ant crawling across an eye; his photo of Hujar, dead, eyes still open. Hujar's photo of Thek in a catacomb, his head flanked by skulls with cavernous sockets, staring down the barrel of the camera; his photograph of Thek masturbating, eyes half closed in ecstatic pleasure. In his *Screen Tests*, as in all of Warhol's series, he stares at the camera for four minutes at sixteen frames-per-second. In Thek's *The Tomb* (1967), frequently called Death of a Hippie, the life-size effigy — Thek, The Hippy — has his eyes closed, but sticks his tongue out.

*

> That discourse one might call the poetry of transgression is also knowledge.
> He who transgresses not only breaks a rule.

> He goes somewhere that the others are not;
> and he knows something the others don't know.
> — Georges Bataille, *Story of the Eye*

*

Halley's Comet, the only known short-period comet that is regularly visible to the naked eye from Earth, last appeared in the inner parts of the Solar System in 1986; Halley will next appear in mid-2061.

It is the only known comet that can reasonably be seen twice in a lifetime.

*

Louis Shankar

ocular frieze (eye with moon with mars)

the winter full moon
and inside the withered tree
three sticks of bamboo

          Harry Gilonis

wet sky of full eye
and within moon occults war
you too can't be blinked away

          Amy Evans Bauer

kangetsu ya
kareki no naka no
take san-kan

          Yosa Buson

—07.12.22
year's last full moon, lunar occultation of Mars, Arctic air brings greater visibility

Untitled (womb with comet)

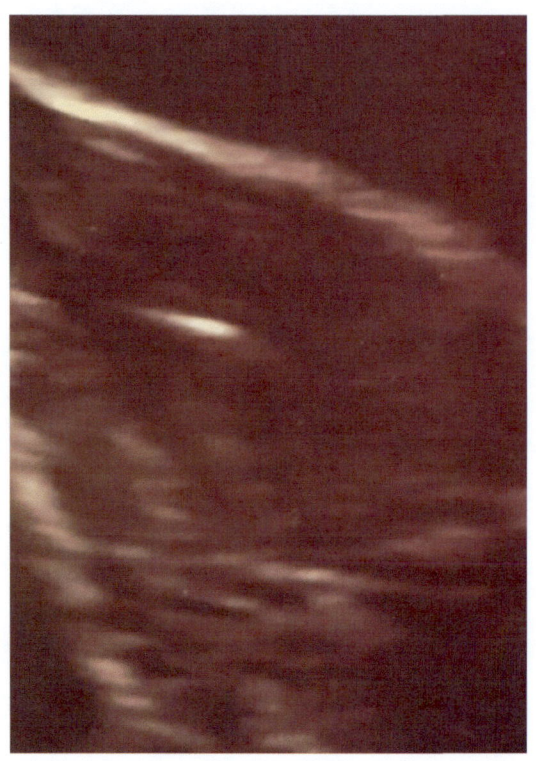

Untitled (womb with second comet)

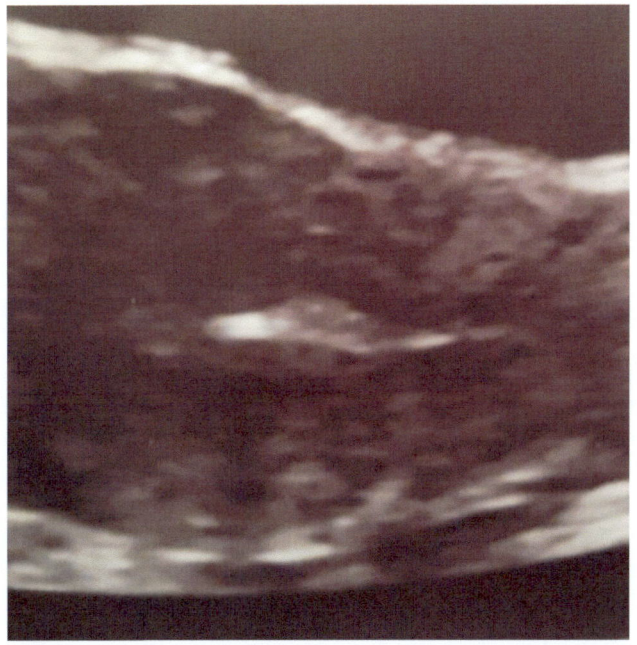

Amy Evans Bauer

I see babies

Here, in this – this pause – I catch silence. Two people are standing on a rooftop. The concrete is covered in a moss that won't shift even in the heaviest of rains. It is prehistoric compared to the fizzing beer in his hand and the polyester in my coat. This is the coming together of time, as it meets over and over like the most ordinary thing in the world. The moment is romantic in the way a rooftop at night in a city can be for a person who has never been unhappy. But I turn my face from the romance like it's hot steam from an oven – makes my eyes run – and instead I turn my eyes upright, looking for lights. He thinks about kissing me. I think about shooting stars – two things that last forever if they matter enough.

We are here because he's alone. I am here because you are with me, and he doesn't even know.

II

I found out that I was pregnant on a Sunday. Tipped the candle from an empty jam jar full of wax onto the bathroom floor of the pub and filled it with my piss. Dipped four plastic tests into it and stood there, waiting.

II

Before you, life was a flash. A bus hurtling by. A sneeze. A thing of lightning-fast conception and completion. Before you, I would have been on this roof, alone with a stranger. My 'I' was just that. A single line on a page and a single line on a pregnancy test. Before you, my 'I' hadn't split open to reveal a 'we' I'd not been before. Split open to reveal an egg with two yolks.

Now 'I' am forever gone. 'I' will never come back. Together, we are plurality and multiplicity within a body. We are a disease or a virus. An expansion.

II

My Dad chose my middle name from the country I was born and the day I arrived – as the glimmer of Hale Bop Comet shot across the Welsh sky – when my scream into existence scored the whir of hot fire across the death of that early spring. Where does the origin of a story live? Where does a life begin? A cave somewhere? A hole? All those little stumbling lambs skinned in the night.

Seren means star. I carry it with me in the back of my throat, on my ID cards, like a glittering brooch at a house party, as I introduce myself to strangers. Hattie Seren May Morrison. I roll the 'r' so they ask me more questions. *Where are you from?*

You were meant to arrive next May. I was meant to squeeze you out like a seed from a pod. The opening of a new eye. The start of my new 'I'. Blue and purple. Raw. Ridiculous.

II

Do you know what confirmation bias is? I learned about it while standing at a bus stop in Shepherd's Bush a few years ago. It's when you start believing in something and then you find proof of it everywhere. Like death. Like ghosts. Like angel numbers. II. I'd never noticed the blue and red coaches that rally between Oxford and London until I started to take them regularly as a nineteen year old, listening to folk music and being the kind of person who wore opinions like jewellery. *I never want to have children*—I'd lie unprompted - *it's a death sentence.*

I remember turning to a boyfriend and saying *these buses are everywhere, aren't they? How have I never seen them before?*

But now, instead of buses, I see babies. Round ones with mossy hair. Slimy ones with disappointment already in their pursed lips. On every street and park bench. Long ones with curly toes and worry. Kicking ones with skin like flaking pastry. I see their fingernails. I see their faces.

I see you.

II

Standing in the hallway of my hazey, nauseous fever dreams, I watch you play musical statues with your eyes on me – Mum, Mum, look Mummmmm that word is too heavy for me to carry, my fingers slip, I stutter – but as your body stills, your growth does too, your breath is held long and heavy for too long, and you purple, harden– you wave, you disappear.

A cloud of smoke eases into the sky.
What do you think they'll do with, you know -
There will be a cremation at a cemetery and you may arrange a ceremony if you wish.
It makes me wince to think of you, outside of me like air I can't inhale again. Makes me feel like I'm living in an apartment with all of the furniture missing. Makes me want to go somewhere very far away from my body.

II

I wish forward, through time, to us. Us and death. Us and nurses. Us and blue sheets and scans and waves and tight eyes crying and tissue boxes and the blood that would not stop until one day, it just
did.

I wish forward. I rush forward, with you as a passenger. We are on fire together. We are incinerated.

Forgive me for giving us up. *Give me up.* Give up.
Look up.

II

Look, a shooting star.

What did you wish for?

Hattie Morrison

Sammy Paloma

Power Up!

I can be powered by dominoes and blue cheese
Côtes du Rhône and Chablis
and that shit you saved for cooking

I can be powered by honesty boxes and soft clouds
jump scares and secret fastjets
with code names like *X32a* and *Slow Doris*

I can be powered by nitrogen bubbles
when I've stayed too long
by rocket sleds and loose fillings
bare legs, corsets, coronations
that electrical snap when you touch my arm

I can be powered by nostalgia and DRM
Morrisey and Michael Jackson
at least until 1989

I can be powered by wet dreams and toothless birds
gravy that
drips
down
sundays

I can be powered by history porn and the gilded cage
those untested bombs with yields of 50 megatons
now I am become death

I can be powered by robert ludlum and dan brown
those scandi salt and pepper shakers you paid too much for on ebay
all sorts of prescriptions and sometimes none

I can be powered by anything
brought down by it all

Blind Spot

Come
mysterious
starling.
Come
Lord Howe
gerygone.
Fly.

In Search of Lost Time

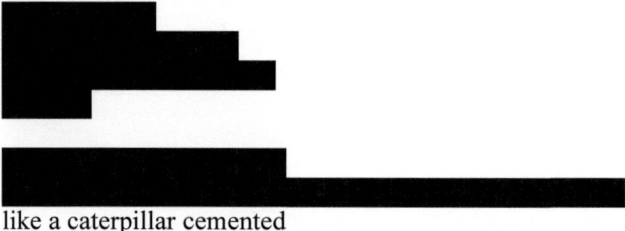

like a caterpillar cemented   safely in its cocoon

Forever, machine

Grumble grumble grumble,
Grumble grumble grumble,
Grumble grumble grumble,

Grumble grumble grumble,
Grumble grumble grumble, bang.

AN Grace

Coup d'oeil du théâtre de Besançon, the engraving by Claude Nicolas-Ledoux that probably inspired Paul Thek's painting, was published for the first time in 1804, just before Ledoux died in relative obscurity, having been imprisoned during the revolution and then sidelined as a suspect vestige of the Ancien Régime. His Wikipedia page features the sections "Difficult times" and "Utopianism". It's not hard to imagine his appeal to Thek.

Ledoux's image turns on a confusion between inside and outside or artist and work, on a strange and incomplete inversion of an eye staring out and a theatre shining back. A beam of light that might otherwise simply be a spotlight illuminating the architect's auditorium as it appears reflected in the pupil (Ledoux's?), pours out from bottom of the eye, and so seems to be emanating from beneath the eyelid. It's an image divine and theatrical, godlike and campy.

Thek picks up on Ledoux's neoclassical, visionary trippiness, simultaneously exaggerating and deflating it, flattening the image out in clashing yellow and violet paint, flicking out the eyelashes, and replacing the ethereal glow with one of his favourite motifs, the comet. What are we looking at/what's looking back at us here? In 1960, years before he met Thek in Rome, Brion Gysin wrote that "Art is the tail of a comet". Perhaps this is Thek looking back at his art, his career and his life as a brilliant shooting star/self-consuming trail of disaster, at once distant and painfully close to home.

The kind of partial, failed or reversible inversion, the unsettled bringing together of opposites in Ledoux's engraving is a movement that runs through Thek's work like a compulsive tic, and is part of what makes it so appealing. It's most famously visible in Thek's meat pieces, where nice perspex vitrines and hi-tech cubes were filled with putrid flesh. A perverse dig at the precious and macho perfectionism of minimalism, say lots of catalogue essays, and this rings true enough. But when he stuffs one of Andy Warhol's Brillo Boxes with red meat, responding to Drella's fetish for flat surfaces with a hunk of deep tissue, it looks more like something else. A joke, obviously, but also homoerotic play with someone who didn't necessarily play well with others, and an act of queer solidarity between two artists: I'm a freak, too.

A Document Made by Paul Thek and Edwin Klein, published alongside Thek's 1969 exhibition with the Artist's Co-op at the Stedelijk and the Moderna Museet, does anything but document the show. Instead, it features a kaleidoscopic photo-collaged mise-en-abyme of Thek and his friends and lovers fucking around in their Amsterdam studios, short-circuiting the production-oriented temporality of the studio into open-ended or endless fun. At the actual exhibition, Thek bought his dead effigy back to life, and chairs were placed on top of tables. The utopian-sounding Artist's Co-op was represented by a chicken coop, complete with live chickens.

A kind of ethics emerges from this relentless and contrarian practice of punning, of flipping things around and reflecting them back on themselves, an ethics which becomes particularly explicit in the often-allegoric newspaper paintings. *Apotheosis of the Titanic, The Tower of Babel as Vortex*: catastrophe as consecration, collapse as communion. This was obviously linked to Thek's religion and his reading of scripture, the latter channelled and updated for Reagan's AIDS epidemic: *Comfort the afflicted/Afflict the Comfortable*.

A series of engravings that Thek made in Paris in 1975 features motifs similar to those in the newspaper paintings, including the eye/comet pairing. Appropriately enough, half of them came out backwards as he got to grips with the process. In one, a pair of banners interlaced with a comet float among fluffy celestial clouds. In place of the divine tautology "I AM THAT I AM" that Brion Gysin had permutated out into further meaningless on BBC radio a decade earlier, Thek offres a bratty "I AM AM I?". Another etching shows a large X, flanked by falling comets and featuring the inscription: "THE CROSS OF POLLYANNA AND CASANDRA/THE 'GOOD' vs THE 'TRUE!'" This seems to have been Paul Thek's cross to bear: an insufferable love of even the most saccharine beauty, and an inability not to put things as he saw them, often bitterly, even if it meant alienating collectors, friends, and lovers.

In a letter written to Peter Hujar on 30 August 1968, Thek laments (ironically? sincerely?) the marriage of one of Hujar's former partners to a woman: "I mean queer has a purpose and it seems morally wrong to me not to sleep with members of one's own sex too. I mean hedonism and love are the only way." Queer has a purpose, though alongside love, sex and hedonism (obviously), Thek's work suggests that this purpose might also involve being at once Pollyanna and Cassandra: too much sweetness and too much bitterness to swallow easily, relentlessly turning ideas, myths and platitudes backwards and inwards in order to find something better or truer, as a survival reflex, for a laugh, and as an act of faith.

James Horton

Fragments from the annex

An inconsistency appears—an untitled error—a bowl of cherries becomes unknown to you; distant or invisible

I see you for twenty-five minutes a week dripping with extra-terrestrial dust and a cosmic atmosphere. You feathered orbit. You gestured form—with all grace left at the fringes of the door. I'm a curve ball

Phosphoric acid on the hands and in the crevices right behind my knees. Planting enough bulbs to be seen from space. Plant enough to hurt not only your hands but your forearms and shoulders. Think about Sylvia Plath's disdain for flowers whilst wondering if the pile of phosphogypsum can also be seen from space. Phosphogypsum; a byproduct from the production of fertilizer – a barren eerie radioactive slither. And by slither, I mean one of many thousands of cracks at the very end

Also wondering if you want to hang out sometime. Also wondering what John Ashbery means by describing the day as 'fudge dark'. Wondering if it's even actually that fun to listen to jazz. Wondering if you're just done now

Noting an acute bleakness but I like your shoes

Dust. Dust. Dust. Dust.

The cosmos is spent. Spade to fork we leaver and remove the forms out, but it's fallen and rooted all the way down the now, thick and woody stems. It takes a while to shift through the verdure and decay. You've formed your own rules on how tall and fast you want to grow. You'll hold tightly onto a vigorous decline. Cling onto your own network – a subsoil tangle. Text you that I'm working in a Delacroix painting (The Death of Sardanapalus, 1846). And it's the last flourish of life. And the recently deceased. And the very much left a while ago. A senescent chorus. Not much of a silence

A fundamental harshness of light. We close the blinds. You're sweating like clingfilmed ham. Beaded down your back. How do you dance if you sweat this much? The stage is a damp ocean and an endless puddle as dangerous to you as it is to others. It's just a gossamer shine. Transferred from one body to another. Cold sweats on a warm day. I pass you a towel because you're ill. You're an unseasonably warm October. You're the record-breaking temperatures across Europe. You're even a dry April right now. Even a drought. And most definitely the deluge once the weather breaks

Oh I'm here am I? Where to now? I had been growing. They had been growing. A pluperfect continuous (jargon) or a complete (common) plate fragment. Describe something small but vital. A snapshot of many distorted by dark matter. A feeling (or two). A deep drop down and back again. You're standing there in all your multiplicities - a stagnation of time laid bare - thatched and sorted. Put on your coat and we'll leave. Come back in a year or two and pose in all our heat but just that little bit smaller. We'll waste away. We all do out here, feel our bodies a little more each year. Bend down and smell the earth – like chocolate pudding

Says he doesn't want to become one of your stories, just a soft silvery lover remembered fondly. Piss-wet through by 9am. He made a cabinet from oak stolen from the owners of the house. One hundred and nine dovetail joints all cut by hand – 'I was seeing dovetails in my sleep!' he exclaimed and I sat so deep in the dual meaning for a while. Green dick. Dicky meadows. A potential wood of willows sits over winter in dark dark soil. An abstract beating of strings via words via hands via flesh and muscle

Not quite sure why we made out. You can make me feel bad if you want to but it doesn't take away the fact that it was your idea. My bones are swelling as I lay supine on the bedroom floor

(Like Arthur Russel) A young man sits on the bridge after nightfall, like Emily Dickinson – finish on finite infinity

Nick Wood

Inventory of Infinitums

I have no desire to conquer anything. It matters to me enormously that I am well-liked. My dreams do not involve narrative but increasingly involve me, furtively looking for somewhere to masturbate.

The first time I read this line by Clarice Lispector it knocked the breath out of me:

"What colour is the spatial infinity? It is the colour of air."[1]

The second time I read this line I thought about vision, sublimity, the density of all the air in front of my face stacked up on top of itself. The third time I read this line I realised that the first two times, I'd been reading the words in the wrong order. The sentence re-arranges itself like a distance already elucidated. *What is the colour of spatial infinity?* A misreading. The horizon has shifted in the sentence.

When all the air in front of the face is stacked on top of itself, after several many miles it turns deeply electric blue-indigio-black. Spatial infinity is the colour of invisible air, and this is colour of density. This sky is a vast series of layers that subsume the other, from invisibility to saturation-point. This colour of spatial infinity is that of something unknown, untitled. Or perhaps, the spatial infinity is in the texture, the weight, the breath – something to feel a part of, move with.

The colour of spatial infinity is not obfuscated, but is ever-shifting, in-motion, wherever the eye settles. This colour is the distance from the pupil to the closest star. Describing the thing in front of you, indefinite. Otherwise known as: the freedom that comes with not-naming, (Untitled), leaving room for infinity.

* * *

The differences between a comet and a shooting star are directional. Shooting stars are grains of dust or rock that burn up as they enter the earth's atmosphere.[2] A comet is a ball of ice and dirt that orbits the sun. When heat from the sun vaporises the ice, the resultant escaping gas propels the comet away from the sun and it is here that it produces its 'tail'. The word 'comet' comes from the greek, meaning *long-haired star*. I think there is a *Simpsons* episode about them. Once every five years, on estimate, it's possible to see a comet from earth with the naked eye.[3]

In *Bart's Comet*,[4] this cosmic snowball is discovered quite by chance, shooting towards Springfield at lightning speed. As the townspeople huddle together in a bunker, the comet blazes in the night sky like a second sun. Here, the Simpsons have to contend with their ashen fate, and are made to confront the violence of sublimity.

When Kant speaks of the sublime he speaks with a co-mingling of enjoyment and horror – staring into a great distance or at something more massive and powerful than the fragility of a body. "*The description of raging storm, or Milton's portrayal of the infernal kingdom,*"[5] Kant's sublime speaks of scale, something with speed, sound, heat. Direction and force. The sublime is bigger than the beautiful; "*valleys with winding brooks and covered with grazing flocks, the description of Elysium, or Homer's portrayal of the girdle of Venus.*" Kant's beautiful and sublime speak to an allegory for a "*patriarchal (but not necessarily male) conquering of subject.*"[6] A measurable magnitude by which natural phenomena and bodies can be said to be surmounted, or surmountable.

I feel no desire to conquer these comets.

Look instead, towards Lispector's infinity. She turns away from Kantian sublimity with a kind of *ad-infinitum* embracing of the undefinable. The sublime is already in the air in the lungs, part of the body, and this has nothing to do with scaling a great invincible face, or girdle. Just looking a little longer, breathing together.

> "*I want, inside this night, life raw and bloody and full of saliva. I want this word: splendidness, splendidness is the fruit in its*

succulence, fruit without sadness. I want distances. My wild intuition about myself. But my main thing is always hidden."[7]

This is what infinity means when it says the colour of air is untitled. I turn to *splendidness* instead of the sublime: this vast interior world of nameless distances. My main thing always hidden.

This splendidness looks into the massive indigo sky with one big eye wide open and watches it like wet paint dripping back into its own hole. In this bloody night the stars cave in on themselves and rain spits in puddles, throws the sky back at itself. These fruits, fires, infernal snowballs reflected massively from silver stars to the ripped-open insides of crips packets glittering together. This splendidness witnesses a thread of the world stuck the eye. Direction unknown, yet orbital.

* * *

An image of Halley's Comet taken in 1986,[8] shows a bright white slash across deep blue spatial infinity. The image goes black, deep blue, electric blue, burning white. It burns a hole in the screen, a hole in the blue, scatters itself hotly across the sky, eye wide, wider.

One evening dense in smoke and dusty light my friends agree that *Low* is David Bowie's best album. As we say this, *Sound and Vision* swirls sluggishly, scatters like stardust like the ash on the table, *"blue blue electric blue."*[9] Colour of my room. Pale blinds drawn all day.

Comets wrap the air with their electric aether. This blue, blue electric, like the sky ablaze in gaze and light. Gazing, like glazing, involves something liquid, dripping thick indigo or the fluid-heavy infinitum of the sky downward to dark puddles, blinds drawn all day, crisp packets, stars.

These materialities arrange themselves thusly – thread on a spool. A drawing of a planet. A hole. Eating one's own tail.

* * *

It is Homer Simpson, America's dearly loved doofus, who answers to the sublime. Against the background of life in the comet-proof bunker growing ever-more sordid, Homer assures his children that when the comet reaches Springfield, it will have burnt up to the nonthreatening size of a Chihuahua's head. They leave the bunker and watch the comet hurtle towards earth. When his son clenches this ball of dirt in his hot yellow hand, that which is bigger than him, godfearing Homer Simpson and his brood become a conduit for a kind of infinity. A distance not conquered but simply travelled, for *"everything that is never began,"*[10] eternal.

A comet, then, wandered but not conquered, one part of the sky slashing the pupil the eye the I, watching it leave, ad-infinitum. Wanting, watching it leave trails.

In the opening sequence to *Bart's Comet*, Bart writes on his classroom blackboard one thousand times, *"Cursive writing does not mean what I think it does."* It means something else then, something unwritten because Bart is captured mid-thousandth-sentence, which is without end, without knowing. The writers of the show never told him what cursive does mean – we are left looking.

To leave this thing looking, untitled is to open it, like an inventory of infinitums. Endlessness. An inventory of things which do not title themselves, nor you. This is to leave the whole thing in-motion, electrified. Living.

References

[1] Clarice Lispector, *Água Viva*, 9th edn (London, UK: Penguin Classics, 1973) p.18

[2] *Meteor Showers and their Relation to Comets*, 1999
https://www.astro.umd.edu. [accessed 13/11/22]

[3] Tim Reyes, *When is the next great comet?* 2020
www.earthsky.org/space/northern-hemisphere-overdue-for-a-great-comet/ [accessed 20/11/22]

[4] 'Bart's Comet', *The Simpsons*, S.6, E.14, dir. Bob Anderson, 1995
https://simpsonswiki.com/wiki/Bart%27s_Comet [accessed 05/12/22]

[5] Immanuel Kant, *Observations on the Feeling of the Beautiful and Sublime*, trans. by John T. Goldthwait, (Berkeley and Los Angeles, CA: University of California Press, 1764) p.47

[6] Barbara Claire Freeman, *The Feminine Sublime: Gender and Excess in Women's Fiction* (Oakland, CA: University of California Press, 1997), p. 4.

[7] Lispector, p.18

[8] *Photos of Halley's Comet Through History*, 2011
www.space.com/11552-photos-halleys-comet-images-astronomy.html [accessed 13/11/22]

[9] David Bowie, 'Sound and Vision', *Low*, (RCA Records, 1977)

[10] Lispector, p.19

Bart's Comet, *The Simpsons*, (S6 E14), dir. Bob Anderson (1995)
www.simpsonswiki.com/wiki/Bart%27s_Comet [Accessed 05/12/22]

Sophie Paul

tendon
after Paul Thek's Untitled (eye with comet) c. 1985

1.   See *not* a comet, but a tendon drawn across the iris's diameter, sinew obstructing its gaze. Bashful interior strung and stuck, like rheum sleep unable to weep away.

Joining mineral to thew, connective tissue sits at a half-way between our living, breathing muscles and our dead, ossifying skeletons. It is mostly inert, and with the brute exception of bone, it is the last to rot.

Unlike the tactility of skin, the carnality of flesh, the fine networks of our nervous systems, what visions might we conjure up if we took tendons, sinews, ligaments as synecdoche for the modern body? Elastic, fibrous — at once intimate and impersonal. Our forms in disjunction become a tangled snarl of wires, or fabric woven and thrumming.

2.   In 2020, I developed acute tendonitis in my right arm as a result of spending too long at my desk. Unable to afford private physiotherapy and stuck for too long at the bottom of a pandemic waiting list, the whole appendage became almost unusable for several weeks. My flatmate had to help me dress and undress every day.

They still call it tennis elbow (it being lateral epicondylitis), evoking quaint images of a leisurely pastime taken a touch too far. However, these days, the condition is most commonly caused by working long hours at a computer.

The tendonitis isn't the first injury affecting this limb; when I was 14, I shattered my wrist falling off a wall, and at 17, I burned the skin on the back of my hand playing fast and loose with a camping stove. Yet, while bones break under impact, flesh tears and warps from sharp and sting, connective tissue is perhaps unique in that it is most often ground down by the mundane routines of industrial life.

Injuries of repetition.

See, another piece of Thek. Turn over dear Andy's brillo box. Beneath its colourful veneer of convenience: sinew and strain. This piece of meat is the steel wool pad pressed tight between greasy pans and fraying nail beds. Rashy detergent rubbed raw into working fingers. This is the stove that feeds the factory line, that keeps the gaping mouths of its offspring satiated. This is unpaid, reproductive work.

This is elbow grease.

Bones and brawn get too much credit. Anatomical drawings of the human form usually show us standing still, gravity our only contender. But it is our tendons that thanklessly bear the burden of everyday life in motion.

3.   More so than calcareous remains or raw meat, tendon on its own conveys both the rapturous disassembly of the body, and the enduring trauma of an absent whole. No wonder the cinema of body horror so often draws on the imagery of the deep inside, turned out.

And how close the association is with *transmission*.

See, Shinya Tskukamoto's 1989 film *Tetsuo* begin with a man (described as a 'metal fetishist') driving an iron rod into his leg in an act of self-mutilation cum masturbation. He is soon overcome with a mass of proliferating cables and pipes and wires that take over his body, and ultimately lead him to unwittingly kill his partner during sex.

Hardly surprising that the body politic as connective tissue is made to speak the language of perversity, weakness and corruption when we are forced to reside within an economic system that seeks at every juncture to conflate the visibly contingent with failure.

And at the same time, it is a system that tells us "we're all in this together," like I am queuing up behind the ghost of Ronald Reagan for my monkeypox vaccine.

For chosen family ties *are* so much more visible than those nuclear dependencies. Our intimate connectivity is out on show, rendered into a statistic, a risk factor, pathologised. Taken as childish, as base, as dangerous.

And we haven't yet learned what it means to grow old like this, together, because there are so many ties that now lead to nowhere…

a minute's silence

4.	Though I spent weeks flexing my arms with a basketball pressed between my palms, the elbow never fully healed. Eventually, I learned to use the limb in a new way. Despite occasional displacement injuries in my shoulder and wrist, most activities are painless. Still, I never get over the feeling that my arm is now, somehow, an adjunct to the rest of my body.

I remember reading somewhere that you are supposed to look at your palms to tell if you're dreaming or not. But now I wake in the middle of the night and believe for a moment that somebody else has left their hand in my bed. I walk off-centre like I am carrying an invisible heavy load to one side. And when I'm doing the dishes, absent-minded-like, I find myself glaring down at the rubber glove like the whole limb is borrowed from a friend, and then like it is filled with nothing but hot air, expanding rapidly.

Until I realise that what I am experiencing is not absence or separation but simply pain, the stiffening joint protesting my attempts to extend it out of a new gnarled shape that I have come to mistake for comfort.

A pulled tendon is the opposite of a phantom limb, because the offending part is still here even when it pretends not to be. I find myself missing something that remains, the rest of my body having to move differently to compensate. Missing becomes adjustment, accommodation, a neverending act of putting things (back) together.

In this way, the failure of connective tissue reminds me that we were always *in pieces*.

5.   See, there is here tenderness too. Pulled heartstrings. Holding tight gently. Collagen is the most abundant protein in mammals, and we are threaded through this amino acid, knitted against ourselves over and over and over.

My flatmate pulls together the buttons of my shirt, pressing the cheap plastic into their tough threaded housings. "That's you," he says with a wink, pats softly my arm and kisses me on the forehead. "Same time tomorrow? Now back to work."

Jae Vail

Elizabeth Zvonar

That purple feeling

Halfway through the movie, I walk out of the auditorium. As the door closes, the sound sighs away, like a half-heard conversation. The brief interruption of silence in the reception hall causes people to look at me from the ticket counter. A man is having a conversation with the ticket inspector. The conversation resumes when I raise my hand. Nothing wrong. I just want to go home. They don't look at me anymore. They are only concerned with each other. Outside, a few people take shelter under the awning. Heavy rain is forecast for tonight. The foreplay is currently taking place. Brief upsurges of wind gusts sweep through the street. The drizzle is lifted as if it needs to be brought back to the clouds. I look at my watch. Maybe Sam is still awake. He usually lingers in front of the television for several hours after his night shift. Maybe he fancies a beer, somewhere. A few people also step out of the cinema. They slide their umbrellas open and disappear into their collars. I walk back into the hall, towards the controller, who is still standing and talking. When I tap on the glass of his booth, the conversation falls silent. The man looks at me wearily. I point to the red umbrella lying on the floor behind him, then point to myself. He grabs the umbrella from the ground and sticks it out through a hole. The image seems to have come straight out of the movie. I make a list of everything I have unlawfully taken as I cross the road: ashtrays, pencils, glasses, books, clothes, flowers, singlets, notebooks, meals, drinks, sunglasses, shoes, and now an umbrella.

The streets are poorly lit. A metro rocks the rails. There is a crackling sound, followed by a blue flash and the street seems to have been plunged into a thunderstorm for a moment. Sparks are briefly visible, and I wonder what would happen if I caught them, and, with the holes created by the heat, I could make a shower out of my umbrella. The Hudson gives free rein to the wind. It pushes into my back; my steps almost become jumps. I have to be careful not to end up with my entire weight in the puddles. Shop windows light up the street a little as I pass dark figures, tucked away in coats or hidden under newspapers. Parts of the street along the closed Ramrod are cordoned off.

A series of police sirens and ambulances drive by. A group of men stays at the barrier tape to watch officers walk into a house. As I go deeper into the city, more cars drive down Christopher Street. The sharp sound of sirens echoes down the street as the bright colors of flashing lights illuminate the road surface. A man on the porch of his shop shrugs his shoulders when we make eye contact. This, too, is part of it, he seems to say, the endless flare-up of violence, the boys fighting with each other, the dull thump when a foot wants to enter a belly, the howl of a girlfriend at the sight of blood, the indifferent reaction of anyone with an appointment or money. Keep watching or get the hell out; sooner or later the street in front of you will be blocked off by a platoon of cops, and your mother will have another anecdote for during her coffee break. And if not, the strong arm of the law will gladly lend a hand in the form of a bullet or a heartfelt shove out of the window. Look at Diego; he can tell. Whichever way you look at it, that boy was pushed.

I find Sam in his hand-woven poncho, rolling a cigarette. The flat has no central heating, so he regularly converts his living room into a huge pillow and blanket fortress. It's temporary, he adds, but my mother never used to allow this, so I see no reason to clean it up again. Sam is a visual artist, and his work consists of large, stringy canvases on which gray or brownish colors, often matte or pastel, predominate. His most recent canvas, called "Man as Landscape", shows an abstract human figure surrounded by swift lines of dark paint. It is an attempt, he says, to break free from the desires in which we find ourselves. The lines resemble ropes to which the figure is chained. Movement is interrupted; the figure's humanity is lifted. The longer I look at the canvas, the more a certain uneasy feeling settles in my throat. I ask Sam if he will turn the canvas over when we go to bed later. He smiles. "What a great compliment! Of course, I will." I grab a towel from the kitchen and dry my shoes. On the television, I hear a commercial for canned soup go by, and I hear Sam laughing out loud at the jingle. For a moment we are together again, and this room is not a battlefield or temporary shelter, but a place of living together. I crawl next to him on the sofa. The rain has stopped.

Lars Meijer

Fool's fire

Ice tips everything in December The
magpies challenging notions
Of the mental realm Gather every
shiny bit we forgot
to remember

Dinosaurs died by fire why
not we? All balanced in the
great Ball of Existence Fate-Lottery
Lactic acid in the body an echo
of the beginning of all life on earth

When we burn it connect to
the microbes, You're no different
from the smallest things but
we've been told the great myth
Of measuring everything against ourselves

& Three cheers for fermentation
The catalyst for all Begging
the question of Where did the sugar
come from in the first place? And
the recent human violence in its name

to refine And fine, I've seen a star
up close in the fire pit and contained in
the firefly palmed to my eye but
as you tell it the story goes Once upon
a time Human looked up and

forgot to remember the ground
Is in the sky too

Clay AD

Transcription (For Joana)

"I seem to teeter on the brink of 'enlightenment' yet my energy is sapped at the root by my awareness of serving two masters, with its traditional result, alienation from everything."
— Paul Thek

Paul Thek was torn between worldly and ascetic desire, between embodied sensuality and a path to transcendence. His desire to return art to its liturgical function is reflected in several works. Paul Thek was an expert on Meister Eckhart. Accordingly, he knew that one must extinguish the self in order to admit light. Thek achieved this state of receptivity through the act of transcription.

The drawing opposite, *Transcription (For Joana),* is the result of several transcription processes. A kind of liturgical drawing. Various motifs were transferred to other drawing surfaces by means of a blue graphite paper. What is shown here is therefore only the intermediate space between the original motif and the copy.

Michel Kessler

Coma

'For some day I'll return'
—from the song *Don't Let the Stars Get in Your Eyes* by Slim Willet

Before the retinitis and total darkness, I saw
the mermaid star, her swishy tail and lavish tresses
waving in the unforgiving night. Too flashy,
some said. I made a wish. Do I have to tell you
what I asked? Yes, that's it: To will the old days
back into existence, a present tense livened
by the anonymous and lust's lubricants, sweat
and spit and cum, in ample supply. I'll summon
the celestial valet, a hunk if ever there was one,
to bring up plenty of ice and dust, ingredients
of the dimming glint in my eye. That way, when
I'm extinguished and speeding toward the sun,
I'll burn myself into a last burst of blinding light,
a memory traced in acrylic and wistfulness.

●

coma *n.* the head of a comet consisting of a cloud of gas
and dust and usually containing a nucleus

●

Short-period comets take less than 200 years to orbit the sun;
in many cases their appearance is predictable because they have
passed by before.   —from the NASA.gov Website

•

It's in my blood—the old ways of telling about the Earth
and stars and their birth, how this all came to be. So, before
the syndrome plunders my memory, I will tell you
how we got where we are. A syndicate of Toltec gods
gathered to decide who would light this time of the Fifth Sun,

which we call *now*. It would be Tēcciztēcatl, that fabulously rich
and desirable dandy—he would illuminate the world by diving
into a raging pyre. He was dressed for the flaming occasion,
dripping in gold and hummingbird feathers and coral and obsidian.
But he loved himself too much—pride would not let him leap.

So it was left to the ungilded, humble, and scabrous Nanāhuātzin,
who did not hesitate. Some day, we, the consumptive, the familiar,
the forgotten, will return. We will be gifted another orbit,
one more chance to light the vastness, another time to dream.

Pablo Miguel Martínez

Emma Harris

Dylan, Unfortunately

"Let me tell you who I am George Joseph Thek but Paul to you
and Paul to me you would have to be me to know why I am
Paul after all this erroneous George business."
- Paul Thek, in a letter to Peter Harvey

After all this erroneous Eileening even in spite of being
held aloft like a World Cup champion during Dexy's
Midnight Runners—

I seek a new burst of music to herald a comet-bright
longing a body re-moulding itself around a half-
remembered dream–

Indeed I dream I have two names one when I'm looking
forward straight into the muck of life and another when
I'm looking up at the sky—

Then pluck a name from the depths of sea Dylan with its
salt and moss uncolouring under overcast skies and an
acclaimed singer I've only ever a passing interest in—

But I have been Dylan in every story I've told about myself
for these fifteen years Dylan in every script imagining myself Drew
Barrymore-bashful and kissed and kissed Dylan in every video
game clasping every Pokéball and tending to every pixelated
Chrysanthemum—

I will be Dylan every time I eat a limp cheese sandwich
Dylan when I run out of battery Dylan even if the
government says I'm not Dylan wearing too many layers
Dylan imperfectly explaining my sexuality Dylan with my
fifth cold of the year Dylan when it's all over Dylan when
I'm ice cream for the worms Dylan when I don't have
change for a tip Dylan when my braver siblings name

themselves Soda or Chartreuse Dylan eavesdropping on the train Dylan affixed in the beam of stares curious confused and hateful Dylan in cowardice Dylan in constipation Dylan to you though always a little afraid you might un-Dylan me—

What a glory, to me myself all over every future mistake—

You would have to be me to know why I am Dylan in the midst of all this erroneous business.

Dylan McNulty-Holmes

in storage

You can smuggle a lot into a painting:
figs
violets
vines
ink
bruises
canterbury bells
a thundering night sky
a purple lost boy wishing on a star.

At least we can be confident of that. If nothing else, at least we can be confident that we can deposit purple boys into paintings.

If the world stares at you, stare back, and if you have to hide do it inside a painting.

Maybe he knew that as he sat in his New York apartment, coating canvas in purple. That he could make a flat surface give way. That he could open up a space just big enough
to enter
into.[1]

His sculptures were crafted from 'highly perishable materials'[2] decomposing in the here and now, but his paintings were different.

Acrylic rooms in which to wait out years.

All the boys are still in the paintings somewhere. They are waiting in paintings.

Like parents, we wait up for them.

───────────────

[1] Hisham Matar, *A Month in Siena* (2019)

[2] https://whitney.org/exhibitions/paul-thek, accessed: 28.11.22.

So when you've spent the afternoon sitting on a bench in the Whitney or wherever, make sure you rise softly. Walk with care across the gallery floor and out of sight, until the automatic lights blink off. But let the door stand ajar.

The boys will emerge, drenched purple and vibrant, stretching in the cool dark of today.

Kitya Mark

Rogue at June's End

My eyes are liquid flesh.

Since, we could not have it.

Look into the eye and tell: I am not more

Than liquid nor flesh but the hybridised

Mechanism possessing mechanics

To call itself, if not grow, Anew.

Not 'to be', not to make an 'ontologically'

Savvy sign, nor to make friends

With the rotten every, but to be

A crude reactant to daily life. Reticence.

On the street, on every street, one person

Is bound to cease at a point. They look

Around. They miss the ground.

Even if not the imaginary anything

Could. Called it: here.

Here we called it. Flesh, this pulsing

Surface – I know it is a surface, it is new and always

Changing, unthinking, reticence, it never tells

More or gives nouns – this surface grants

None other than one perfectible sign.

Problem Play

Why is human behavior

Not an eye? Every day

I stunt to write my ethics.

Not waiting I wait

Kindness to yield for presence. I yield.

I have never felt anger I have never felt
The crisp rage at total end. A leg's

Abstention. Obstinate. Anger is

The unmanageable surface. Cressida. I have

Been described as contractual
But I have never laid down terms

For anything

I am quick

For anything

Moulding

We laugh for death because
The eye does not speak.

If the river
goes to
a point
visible to
no human
eye, might

I hold up
My frogged-dignity
and aspect-like
Stupor today? Crisp.

Or, just dogged. If
not day?
If wrong
To listen to

– well, drawing, but
Also. Death-gone
sprawl. Antagonistic
Lilt-like. Garnet-driven.

Katherine Franco

Scotoma

A comet crosses an iris. An eye in the colours of irises. The shooting star's tail opening a wound to bare canvas. White of nothing, blue flecks.

The wound bisects the cornea. So much of Thek's work is about cutting, orchestrated cutting. It expands the terms of collage into the world of objects. This is most explicit in the dismembered traces of *Technological Reliquaries* (1964-1967), but it is also here in *Untitled (eye with comet)* (c. 1985).

Cutting further animates *The Tomb* (1967), a life-size sculpture now lost. Thek's likeness looking down on his own body as he works on it, as documented by Hujar. He is cutting his own figure, enhanced when we hear about the severed hand. It shows up, blackened, in a Google search alongside his waxen recreated face. Thek or his body sliding candidly through the tear between presence and un-presence, agency and non-agency, representation and its other.

Attention to cutting complicates the artist's chastisement of Sontag, which titled her most famous book and earned Thek a dedication: 'Susan, stop, stop. I'm against interpretation. We don't look at art when we interpret it. That's not the way to look at art.'[1] And yet interpretation's cousin, analysis, literalised as dissection, is a violence visited on these works already. Thek's incisions are hysterical, preemptive, self-inflicted: paranoid in a Sedgwickian sense, '*anything you can do (to me) I can do worse*'—and first.[2] If language is most often a way of pulling the world together, art can be a way of exposing the gash.

There's always something feminised about this. Self-harm as an action with layers: dissection, castration and disfigurement all have specific histories with the feminised bodies of living things that aren't straight white men. These bodies must cut open so they can be seen, made intelligible in cross-section. A slice or slash (or sparkle) which traverses the literal and becomes symbolic. It's why the scalpel crosses her eye and not his in *Un Chien Andalou* (1929), the Dalí / Buñuel film. It's why the image prefiguring this cut is a cloud crossing the moon: it does not cross the sun.

A scotoma is an ocular occlusion or alteration first described in nineteenth-century hysteria patients. Doctors studying their women patients record how at the height of their episodes they would experience spots of blindness and other disturbances of vision. Their gazes distorted with their bodies, stiffening and arching in dramatic gestures such as the famous 'rainbow posture'.[3] What is a rainbow but light filtered through water, fire through liquid. The eyelashes, I notice for the first time, in the bleeding watercolours, are wet.

It's not surprising tropes of hysteria would enter the paintings Thek did through the 80s, living through a hyper-exposed and worsening health crisis. They exploit the castration of the gaze; a cut which is not only turned upon the body of the subject but outwards on the world, overwhelming colour, texture, distinction. In the AIDS crisis, the logistics of desire were opening up to their mass-productive reality, the biopolitics of keeping alive people who had had sex, or done drugs, lived lives. It changes worldviews, how we see things politically and personally, however we are positioned in relation to disease. It intervenes in scenography.

An excess of fornication. Another painting in this series is the striking, sexy *Untitled (blue bunnies and red ships)* (c.1984). I want to get my scalpel out and ask if the latter are cops, ambulances or trade. A friend says 'bunny' over 'dick', over 'pussy' because she is a trans girl and prefers specific names for her things. Lots of us died in the crisis too, and we take blue pills in memory of this today. They come to us like many drugs, through a glittering hole in time and research—and with a warning.

When violence is placed upon the subject, it is also placed inside the subject. An eye that opens like legs to history itself: 'with an unquenchable appetite for destruction.'[4] This is an experience of the sublime arising from the warped perspective of risk, and its representation in oppressed groups. Living in the present, with the past. Bodies perceptually, perpetually diseased. The reminder that health outcomes are also narrative outcomes. Who gets to speak is also who gets to feel good and be well. A thing that cannot be unseen, a wound which will not heal. A wet one.

The artwork probes a need to investigate the means of our destruction while not looking away. History happening in full-colour, slow-mo, emo-overwhelm. Watching medication stocks dwindle in favour of more profitable ones from the present series of rolling global crises. These are the surreal conditions in which we are permitted to exist, in a cultural sphere that so fetishises loss. This is a sphere that delights in ephemera, begs a cutting short, a cutting off—because it makes an unlimited resource suddenly finite.

[1] https://bodega-us.org/this-is-my-bodys.html
[2] https://www.ias.edu/sites/default/files/sss/pdfs/Critique/sedgwick-paranoid-reading.pdf
[3] https://www.jstor.org/stable/778984
[4] https://www.jstor.org/stable/3397574

Ainslie Templeton

Susan and Paul as Metaphor: An Opera

Act 1

Narrator:

Susan is deyeing [*sic*]
Paul is deyeing [*sick*]
Everything is a misspelling
Susan and Paul are not talking
Paul is dying before Susan
Therefore, Susan is dedicating
Her book to Paul.

Act 11

Susan:

By metaphor I meant
Nothing more or less
Than the earliest and
Most succinct definition
I know, Aristotle's,
In his *Poetics* (1457b).
"Metaphor," Aristotle wrote,
"Consists in giving the thing
A name that belongs
To something else."

Act 111

Paul:

Like my mom calling me Paul
Or me calling you Susan
Before we stopped talking
Before we became
Too faint to be visible.
Or, for example,
The CDC stating "Cytomegalovirus,
That elliptical genius [*sic*]
Is a Comet
Passing
Slowly
Through the eye."

* Act 11's text is taken from Susan Sontag's *Aids and Its Metaphors*.

Alistair McCartney

Firmament

A borrowed rib
and melodic, bluish

ecstasy. The splendor
of an invented origin,

but I know I wasn't made
that way. The stars

are the only religion
lit from within. I walk

in their heat, glowing
saffron with winter

smoke that's from a fire
or my roaring heart,

sizzling for its lover.
When I was a child

I tried to see myself
but saw nothingness.

Elders decided I shouldn't
tell my secret so I moved

like a little flat stone,
virtuous and barely

grasping the real dreams
of evening. Nightmares

were night mirrors, a kind
of violet sleeping. One day

I woke and some desperate
truth sped over my head,

navigating its own end. All
the continents witnessed

this luxurious spectacle.
Even if I don't, the vastness

remembers.

John Brooks

A wishing well in a casino in Las Vegas takes the form of a fountain. Tiled in green and gold and bordered with fresh flowers, it dominates the foyer. People might throw a couple of dimes in when they pass. Some make a wish. The official line is that they donate the money to charity, but it amounts to so little that the guy who comes to clean it is told to just pocket what's there. After work, he might spend it on a McDonald's or give a dollar to each of his kids.

They had been in Vegas November of last year. They talked each other into booking the tickets one hysterical night at his. Their eyes shone bright with the blue of the laptop screen as they sat on the floor in his bedroom. H had a glass of red wine pressed against his cheek, reading out his credit card number. He shrieked as he clicked confirm.

They'd had an alright time. Looking back, the sheer impulsiveness of the trip was enough of a sign that they were drifting apart. It spoke of their desperation for some kind of excitement. Now he tells people that the diagnosis didn't have much to do with it at all. Vegas was the real wake-up call, Vegas reminded him just how finite time is. This isn't entirely true, but it makes him less sad than going into all the details. He hates describing coming to the realisation that he couldn't keep pushing his body that hard, and how for H, ultimately, it wasn't worth slowing down. He's accepted it now, this need for a gentler kind of joy.

He's glad though that they took the final trip. From the moment they touched down in Paradise, Nevada, everything was bright, harsh, and painfully expensive. Neither of them understood much about gambling, and it turns out it's not as fun if you don't know how poker works. They kind of figured out the slot machines, but even these seemed sly. With so many lights flashing, he felt sure he *was* winning but was so distracted by the blinking neon that he couldn't tell. H spent a lot of time talking to other tourists in the hotel. He tried to charm neighbouring tables when they went out to eat, joking and flirting with the waiting staff, and drank lavishly while asking other patrons to explain the rules of games in a beguiling manner. While H glowed under raucous attention, he became quieter, beginning to worry every time he left to go to the bathroom or fetch a drink that he might return to the sight of his lover pressed against someone else. This idea made him feel relieved, and that concerned him.

His most powerful memory from the trip is of the casino mall. He'd gone alone as H was nursing a hangover and had said something bitter about having no desire to traipse around a capitalistic Disneyland as if that wasn't the whole point of the casino. As if they hadn't been sitting at a bar last night with an honest-to-god money-themed drinks menu (He'd gone for the 'Silver Dollar' - a clear gin-based something which had been very nice actually, not too sweet) He'd spent the whole journey to the mall arguing the unfairness of this comment in his head. Hadn't H understood that to see "capitalistic Disneyland" was precisely why they were there? He'd imagined their presence here as a salient aside, aware of the ridiculousness of the display, but finding a peculiar honesty in this environment and its translation of money in the purest sense. He'd thought he could write an article about it.

By the time he reached the mall, he was angry. He felt stupid for thinking he was seeing some bigger picture and panicked that it had slipped away. H was now somehow a step ahead of him simply by not caring in the first place. The mall remained unchanged. It appeared just as described by the tourist sites: ostentatious with marble pillars and imitation Roman statues. The shops were sunken into faux classical-style architecture with sparkling plate glass windows. The vast domed ceiling painted like a blue sky, loomed above them. It was studded with the 215 Reach Powercore luminaires and 46 ColorBlast Powercore luminaires and performed a sunrise and sunset every day, cycling through bright cyan daytimes to navy nights. You could watch all of this without ever needing to go outside.

The mall was bustling. The closed-in warmth of its fake sky roof felt like a theme park. A Niki Minaj song played over the speakers in the indoor street. Walking into each shop immersed him in a different high-energy pop song, each with a certain BPM, H would have said, to make you spend more. He wondered what the BPM was in the bar last night when H had bought an 80-dollar round. If he was here now he might have said that made him laugh, but he couldn't figure out how to turn it into a joke for later without sounding sharp. The street was at its busiest at 5 pm. Everyone was preparing for the beginning of that day's "sunset". A hen party group were posing, ready for a reliable, mechanical golden hour. Next to them stood a pack of young men in clean trainers, each holding a shiny oversized smartphone, and behind them was an older couple busy getting out their digital cameras to record the spectacle. He overheard someone earnestly telling his partner a rumour that on Tuesdays and Thursdays the patterns were pinker, whereas the rest of the days it was redder, and on Fridays, sunset lasted an extra 15 minutes because there was more footfall. According to this, today would be a pink one. He stopped near a bench and looked up, fighting his embarrassment at being a lone sunset tourist.

At 4:57 the sky was still and blue as ever. He was walking towards the central fountain, constructed out of triumphal arches and marble figures when he noticed a bird drinking the chlorinated water. It looked like a sparrow although he wasn't sure if they had them in America. As he approached, the bird took off, and he stood watching as it looped over the roofs of the shops, then came to rest on a concealed light fitting, casting a shadow onto the edge of the sky. Its wings were surprisingly large against the forced perspective of the clouds. He watched as it shook out its feathers and took off again, realising with surprise that he could hear it calling above the crowd's warm jumble of voices as it shunted against the trompe l'oeil sky. He wondered what it ate, where it slept, and how long it might live.

When it happened, he was still watching the bird. He was considering if the sunsets messed up the bird's circadian rhythm, or whether it got dark enough for the thing to sleep, when, without a sound, the mall plunged into darkness. It happened too fast for anyone to realise what was going on. One second they were seeing, and then seeing was impossible.

In his imagination, the darkness came with a massive sound of a machine whirring off and the cinematic mechanical clunk of something shutting down, but instead there was nothing. The sound system continued to blast pop without disruption. He stood there, disoriented, and realised he was waiting to hear gunshots that never came. A few moments passed. The shoppers' confusion was loud around him. Someone was sobbing, someone else shouting into the darkness, "what's going on? What the hell is going on?". Everywhere, people were lit up by their phone screens, shining torches so that the buildings flickered under bluish circles of light. He looked up to avoid the bright flashes, and let his eyes relax. He thought he could see the eerie white clouds, looming in the great dark ceiling. It seemed hard to imagine it so bright blue under all this darkness. He swore he saw the sparrow then, darting through the room. He thought he felt it pass by his head, a cold rush of wings, more like a bat than a bird. As he turned in search of it, he noticed a rectangle of light ahead of him. Moving closer he saw that somebody had opened an emergency escape, the light stung his eyes, too bright and white. A small crowd had formed before it but it was blocked off by security staff, repeating that they were not permitted to evacuate anyone. It was an electrical fault, they were saying, they were waiting to hear what was going on, everything was fine, and nobody was allowed on the fire escape as they were five stories up. A woman was crying hysterically, begging to get out into the light as others pushed around her. Outside the city looked hot and dry.

Presently the lights came back on. They had missed the start of the sunset and the blue sky was now tinged with pink. Around him people switched off their phone torches and gathered up bags. They smoothed their hair, ran towards friends and companions, and looked back up with relief. Someone, it seemed, had pissed themselves outside of DIOR. An attendant was rushing towards the mess with a mop. A security guard spoke into his radio, frowning while a group of young men in hysterics took pictures of their friend's cream trousers streaked with dark, wet stripes clinging to his legs. He looked back up at the sky. It was a serene, soft pink. The only sign of disruption was the security door which remained slightly open. Outside the sky was still blue.

In Vegas there had been no clocks in the casinos. In fact, it's pretty hard to find a clock anywhere once you start looking. He realised this the other day when his phone died while he was out. He wasn't expecting any calls and had nobody he needed to message, but he felt a deep sense of unease as he carried out his errands. He was acutely aware that he had no idea how fast time was passing, as though the world was running ahead without him.

He hadn't wanted to ask a stranger for the time, and so he was alone in this uncertain state of timelessness. Panic grew in the back of his mouth as he wandered through the city streets. His steps felt helplessly slow and a feeling of lateness rushed through him despite the fact that he had nowhere to go, nothing to be late to. Every door he stepped through brought a fresh pang of fear. The shops were inhospitable, crammed with endless rows of things to be bought but no indication at all of the time.

He began to sweat and mutter under his breath, becoming increasingly irritated at every person walking in front of him. He found his eyes welling up. A sharp terror of wasting time was closing up his throat. By the time he reached the high street, he had broken into a semi-run and would have missed it entirely had he not heard the chimes. Thankfully they were loud enough to break through his panic, and he stopped, looking up towards the sound. He was standing in front of what had once been a church but was now a luxury watch shop. The chimes were coming from the old tower which remained intact, complete with a clock that gleamed like a golden orb in the sky. He had to crane his neck as he stepped backwards from under it, gazing desperately at its face. It was striking half-past three.

Around him people were nipping to the shops or picking up their kids from school, typing in offices or grabbing an afternoon coffee. Standing there, his head tipped back, he began to cry. Tears rolled down his face as the clock's hands shifted serenely round. What was the point of 3:30 pm on a Wednesday? Suddenly exhausted, he felt as though he was giving up on something. He was too tired to walk back but did so anyway and by the time he got home the whole thing seemed ridiculous.

By December the trees are cold and leafless. He's realised that he can see the exact moment the sun sets behind a low building from his kitchen window. He watches it from the hallway, standing with one hand on the light switch. The tungsten bulbs reflect in the pane as the sky slides through pinks and purples to a dusky grey. The lower the sun sinks, the sharper this reflection becomes. He sees red clouds against the corner of a counter, yellow sky cutting through the swan's neck curve of the tap. His upright body casts a shadow in the glass, alert, watching for the precise moment when the sun slips beneath the city. It moves steadily but too slowly to be easily discerned.

As he stands the sun drops through the silhouetted branches and comes to rest briefly on the flat-roofed building. Gradually it sinks lower. Now only a thin coral lip peeps out behind dark brick. His fingers are rigid, and pins and needles buzz in his feet. He blinks, and his heart begins to pound. A hair's width of pink sun remains. His fingers twitch, he doesn't blink. In a single second, the sun vanishes and he hits the switch. The lights plunge. Standing in the dark room, all the pressure falls out of the day. He leans against the doorframe, wishing.

As the last light disappears from the window, the landscape, his house, and himself meld together into a dark flatness. He steps into the kitchen and quietly sits down, resting his hands on the table before him. His fingers are cold and white up to the knuckles. He watches as the beds of his nails darken, turn purple. His skin feels stiff and numb. He looks up out the window again and sees that the streetlamp has switched on without him noticing. He realises he's shivering; it feels as though the purple colour is running up his arms, beating into his chest like its blood.

Jesse Howarth

Fragment on Death

It's like, remember that Claymation movie about Mark Twain?
How he waited for Halley's Comet, how he knew he would die
& ran towards it. It was cosmic like that for him.

Then Huck and Tom and Annie open a door
& enter that strange platform, a desert
suspended in empty space, a placid, generous mask.

It's worth mentioning that Mark Twain never finished that book.
Anyhow the Mysterious Stranger makes the world.
Oh, they are young, they play in the dirt,
the love that simple act of creation,
foreshadowing macking bodies together,
agriculturally speaking.

The desolation meets the sky like a big innocent eye.
Cows, fire. The way trappings of a life
seem so compelling when you're young playing house.
They way they do again when you get older
& death seems so near & a new bath towel
or tart on the counter can stave it off.
& those kids, all they had was the river anyways.

The Mysterious Stranger, Satan, crushes it all,
lightning, flooding, & all that, & the kids cry
& are terrified, run, don't stop running.

The comet approaches, hot, sweating, prescient.
Shit, don't you think you could go out like that?
Knowing just what to do. To say.

jimmy cooper

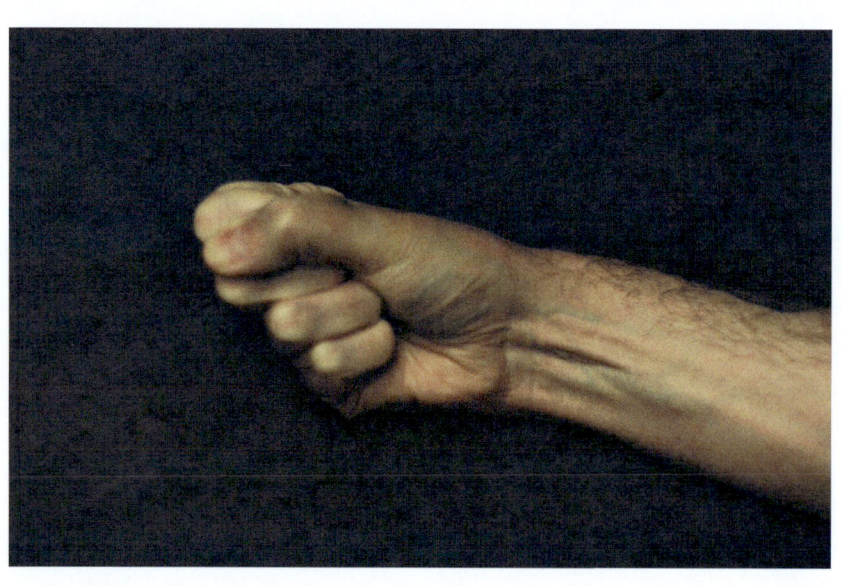

Felix Pilgrim

Light Years

Halley's Comet last appeared in the inner solar system in 1986 and will appear again in 2061. If the comet is a macrocosmic symbol of the human body, do cells—white blood, red blood, viral—similarly circulate in time? Cyclical in their routines of appearance and disappearance, suppression and resurgence, there's something millenarian about them—like Christianity's apocalypse, or Nietzsche's eternal return. Or maybe the image marks a hope for change, the comet a measure of time's passing. If so, it's not a neat marker but a quirky one. Returning every seventy-five to seventy-nine years, Halley's Comet's visits are dependable but not regular. If so, the image anticipates a world that will inevitably be transformed next time the comet penetrates our little circle within the galaxy. A harbinger of an Earth hopefully improved; an Earth without AIDS, perhaps. Paul Thek's painting '*Untitled* (eye with comet)' is dated to circa 1985, ambiguous because it was discovered in a cache after the artist died. I wonder if the speculative dating, or Thek's decision to paint it in the first place, has to do with the furor of press coverage of the impending visit of Halley's Comet. I associate the comet's inexact calendar for its travels with Thek's oscillating choice of materials: with the unscheduled materiality superimposed, in work from this same period, on newsprint, with the artist's interest in both quasi-volcanic eruption and careful framing. Redemption without spirituality or spirituality without redemption? The cosmic exceeds all this, Thek perceived. Awe can inspire awe.

A decade ago I started to learn Ancient Greek. The standard dictionary for this dead language is called *Liddell & Scott*, after its authors. Charles Liddell, an Oxford classicist, was the father of Alice Liddell, model for Lewis Carroll's famous Alice. *Liddell & Scott* remains the go-to dictionary for students of the language. In my recollection, this dictionary contains a word for either "a boy's beautiful eyelashes" or "a beautiful boy's eyelashes." A beautiful boy's beautiful eyelashes? Memory is unreliable. But imagine that: a word for something so specific it reeks of tender attentiveness. Taking the human body's minute, most fragile parts as objects of aesthetic adoration or frank appreciation. I look now through the old heavy book. I've indeed misremembered the word. It's not so gender or part specific: it's καλλιβλέφαρος, kalliblepharos, meaning "with beautiful eyelids or eyes." My always poor Greek is too rusty today to tell you whether the word could be declined into a specifically masculine form. But I like to think in Thek's comet-shrouding eye there's a trace of the ancient, hearty (Whitmanesque?) eroticism relayed by καλλιβλέφαρος.

Scattered around this entry in the lexicon of an unspoken language are other words: for "with beautiful clusters," "with beautiful women," "flowing with beautiful eddies," "with beautiful chariot," "with beautiful reeds." More: "beautifully speaking," "with beautiful girdles," "with beautiful hair or mane." Many of the adjectives refer to horses, many to men. "Beautiful-haired," "with a beautiful spring," "beautiful-shining." The objects or people described by this last adjective must have been stunning in their refulgent and even supernatural spectacle. "Beautifully shaped," "beautifully flowing," "beautiful-cheeked," "with beautiful elbow," "with beautiful leaves." How much more profuse and precise was their vocabulary for beauty than ours? I think of a reply to an Instagram post featuring a beautifully cheeked and elbowed hunk I recently saw: "nghh." Apt enough, but neither poetic nor exact. There is articulacy in the mystery of the unspeakably ravishing, in the swelling inventorying done by Greek adjectives and adverbs. These words poignantly try to name the unnamable.

Beginning in 2010, the astrophysicist Gerard Bodifee—once the director of Belgium's National Planetarium—worked with a scholar of classical antiquity, Michel Berger, to provide names for the thousands of galaxies we humans have come to identify. In the past these were sometimes given elegant Greco-Roman names: just as, in our neighborhood, we had Jupiter and Io, light years away we had Andromeda. Now there are too many, so new discoveries are simply numbered. But Berger & Bodifee wanted to give them all names. Charmingly, they initiated this project to appeal to amateur astronomers. Amateurs love what they study; they like it to have a name, not just a number. Amateurs (from Latin: amare, "to love") deal in bodies (celestial, individual, etc.), not bytes and other numeric data. To one galaxy they gave the name of the Greek word on which I'm fixated. "Calleblépharus Erídani," formerly NGC 1187, has been the site of two supernovas since the 1980s. The astronomer and the classicist named it so because its strange central whorl—comprised of light that is matter devouring itself—resembles an eye. A beautiful eye, at that. The eye of a beautiful boy?

More prosaically, καλλιβλέφαρος also names a species of seaweed. "Beautiful eyelash weed" grows primarily around the coasts of England, Ireland, and Scotland, is dark red, and resembles internal organs. Its dangling nodes evoke eyelashes but have a reproductive function—are part of its "gametangial" body, one that contains both male and female sexual apparatuses. Thek would have enjoyed the compression involved in the shift from galaxy to weed—a miniaturization of the erotically galactic into the banal yet still sensual. Thek's painting doesn't get at the universal through the particular. It does something better, nestling one in the other. The cosmic winks, Thek knew.

Nicholas Chittenden Morgan

Local animals (for Paul Thek)

I am a biotic community
a
    work in process
thinking on modern matters of matter and progress,
what that in mattering really matters, to you and so on —
the monster speaks into the bag of stars —
but, perhaps, I'll
See you soon

Murphy O'Neir

Night Swimming

a Mary Quant blue you could dip your finger into,
stretching out from the first person I, to the third person
She or He or They within a single blink, unscrewing the lid
sometimes just to take a glimpse inside that small white
pot, a deep glittering blue that meant evening, Thursday
evening, a blue that fed into darkness all the way from the
bathroom cabinet to the time when in bed, the grownups
down the path away from the house, outside, the deep
night, dip my finger in there until Thursday evening, that
all all all time, night swimming, the slightest movement of
hands, shoulders, the weight of a body, rolling, separating,
head, legs, torso, glitching in dialogue with all all all
creature words, a voice vibrating down a sentence
following a flickering blue line until it washes up on the
shore, rolling and lapping against the pier, over and over,
a blue purple, drawing back, then no no no she will not
lead an ordinary life, rolling blue black blue naked,
smashing across the sparkling surface of how it was that
she'd been changing the words of her life, and now to
stop, to rest, for the pace to ease, nerves stretched like a
map of the tributaries of a river or the delicate branches of
a tree, as if the notes she was always scribbling on the
back of her hand, an indelible writing, a blue that was
getting nearer, she didn't need to dwell, but to move on,
not to need the old thing so much, almost as if
she *was* energy, and although I always thought of her as of
the earth, that could also have meant moon rock, and so I
had assumed she would live to at least one hundred,
thought she would live forever, even though I had

entertained the idea of her death many times, scaring myself with thoughts of it, but didn't think it would actually happen, no no no and when it turned out she was flesh and blood had become ill even she did not accept it, like Sontag, never gave it the time of day assuming always outwardly at least that she would be better, I loved her for this, for resisting, and then the sense that this was the only way she could describe it, address it, that it was always this, trying to get back to this deep blue purple holding the words, letting them slip slip slip out of the mouth of if offff the tongue, hold them all together, to get hold, let them holddddd, to let them go

Rachel Cattle

Falling in love from near and far

I don't know where Earth begins, or the Sun's surface ends, or how such boundaries are determined, but apparently the photons of light that left the Sun 499 seconds ago have just reached us.

When a comet's course causes it to pass into the Earth's atmosphere it begins to burn, to vaporise. Entering at a low angle it heats gradually and so lights a longer path through the sky.

In New York in the late 90s I first met Thek's work in the flesh: a small show, mostly of his drawings. Love came quickly. It still burns.

Thek's painting from 1985 is crude if compendious: It's a painting of a real comet crossing the path of a human eye seen from a cosmic vantage point.

Thek's painting from 1985 is sophisticated and dreamlike: It's a painting of a fanciful comet burning itself onto an unmoored, infinitely-sighted, symbolic eye.

Either way, or however it might reach us, it is a consummation of human perception and a cosmic perspective.

"I see Earth. It is so beautiful" said Yuri Gagarin in 1961. In 1972 the first image of Earth as seen from space was published; the whole Earth was made visible to everyone.

In 2000 I first saw one of Thek's paintings on paper of the Earth from space. From Thek I learnt that images and objects, don't need to respect edges, rather to honour imagination. Every subsequent experience of his work in any medium seems to bear out that first, baby step of insight.

I'm fashioned, old or new, to think that the experience of seeing/sensing/feeling beauty is akin to seeing/sensing/feeling love. I'm fascinated by humans, dead and alive, that treat love in all its dizzying, joy-and-sorrow-ful plurality as a way of stirring or shaping connection, for unmaking boundaries both imaginary and real, between one and the other and another.

For flesh-made, mortal entities, living in a fractious world of fragile relationships, all manner of attachments matter. Growing connections, or making the edges of things, of ideas, people and activities harder to pinpoint can be the work of love.

Thek is not the only dead person I'm a bit in love with. Giordano Bruno (aka The Nolan) who was put to death in 1600 was a testing, brilliant, disgraced and defrocked Dominican friar turned peripatetic philosopher, mnemotechnical genius and all round Renaissance human with little regard for disciplinary protocols.

Bruno, it seems, was the first person in recorded history to suggest the stars were other suns with planets of their own, and the second that we know of, to hypothesize that the universe extended far beyond the visible and known cosmos and was in fact infinite. He intuited this after realizing that as an observer he harboured a false sense of the centrality of his own perspective: Or as he put it: "In whichever earthly region I should dwell, I see West and East maintaining equal distance..., and wherever you shall go, there will be an equal measure... Therefore the sky is not bounded by a fixed edge."[1] This natural disposition to conflate presence with centrality, he realised, might well hold true on a planetary scale.

Bruno was also an atomist, convinced that everything in the universe was made of the same substance. He proposed, to characterize his position with licence, that if we could all recognise the infinite nature of the universe and understand the divine connectedness of all the matter therein, we would come to respect our deep down sameness. We could abandon our hierarchical ways of thinking and love one another as equals, capable of also fully appreciating our to-be-cherished differences.

Bruno was a very early champion of the new fangled Copernican view of our cosmos. He also believed that space was not only infinitely immense but infinitely sexual too; he wrote of the "amazing embraces" of the Sun and the Earth which he imagines "… can revel in pleasure forever, / Ceaselessly, as her rotation affords her a thousand positions"; comparing the latter to humans for whom "the gentle power of pleasure…/ Breaks forth at once, in only one part of ourselves." Little wonder that he felt, "this sex among gods is of a condition far better."[2]

Bruno had prescient insights on the relativity of observers in space, thoughts on infinity that were centuries ahead of their time. His capacity to appreciate the inter-subjectivity of perspective, and the endless changeability and liveliness of space, and even the sexiness of the universe is beautiful.

Tragically, if unsurprisingly, he was condemned to death and burnt at the stake in 1600.

Thek is an artist who made the fixed edges of things or actions joyously, beautifully, difficult to locate. His work is playful, profound, tragic, and often bizarrely uplifting; it's sexy, celebratory, degraded, and beautiful. The sense of actively surrendering to the generous strangeness of Thek's world is intense. It is the thrill attendant on perpetually negotiating our relationship with space, with spirit, with love, with the world, with the universe, with oblivion. Constructs be damned, I think.

The whole Earth over, we are (perhaps at times only consciously for the length of time it takes for a photon of sunlight to get here, or for a burning comet to cross the path of our gaze), embodied perspectives on space and time. We are all marking it and making it and hopefully staying alert to boundary smudging beauty, the feeling and the work of love.

[1] Paul Richard Blum, Giordano Bruno: An introduction, Rodopi, 2012

[2] Richard Shusterman - Ars Erotica_ Sex and Somaesthetics in the Classical Arts of Love, Cambridge University Press, 2021

Giordano Bruno and Simone Weil comfort Paul Thek, August 10th 1988

Isabel Nolan

The Truth in Painting

I

I was a student
in the analogue daze
when theorists were French
and began with a 'b',
a 'd', or a joke.

I was a reader
of paper, a maker
cutting out letters
to stick on white walls
and fill white spaces.

I owe you the truth
but struggle to care
when 'I owe you' is
always alone, in debt
or indebted.

      II

    Dumb colour
    spills over
    canvas smeared mad
    as God or lashes
    or comets
    so full of
    grit and strokes
    the smell of methylated spirits
    the shade of bruises
    the lack of
    a title. Or frame.

II

The warmth of my fear
has turned it to bitter-
sweet shit. I lick the
purple-gold wrapper:
soft chocolate in foil.

Susan Finlay

poem, content is a small thing

Content is a small thing. Small things matter whether held up close or far away. They accumulate and do big things. The tiniest light left on runs my meter into credit. Tiny numbers tick up like a body count, a life lived, or a mind of memory. You see how it goes: affects accumulate magnetically. Will I always confuse these somethings for everythings, the objects attracted for the force that drew them? I watch the rain bring empty water bottles to swirl at storm-drains they can't pass through. Interpretation is a strange gravity. Think of Donne who saw himself reflected in his lover's eyes like a map of the world. He was a lonely satellite lover. Think of me seeing you reflected in the glaze of your doughnut. The doughnut orbits nothing like a fried meteor in a hollow cosmos. We love the ontology of holes. Affinities reel around lacunae of longing. We are pulled in by extremities of scale and the obvious oscillation between the big and the small. No more questions. No more vertigo. I'm up against it. It doesn't matter what it meant. Rome, the volcano, or the bodies in Palermo. Is the human body an ossuary? Is the human body an orrery? It is not going anywhere. Like meaning, me, or you, who lay supine when Sue, who you once joked you'd marry but it ended badly, came back to you as you lay dying to touch you for the last time and read you poems.

(John Donne, doughnuts, electricity meters, Susan Sontag, Paul Thek)

Ted Simonds

CONSCIOUS FLESH

EXT. BEE HIVES - DAY

CLOSE UP ON SMOKE POURING OVER A WOODEN BEEHIVE.

Loud humming, the buzzing of bees. A gloved hand holds the steel cylinder smoker and the scene undulates gently, following the movements of the smoke over the wooden frame of the hive. The humming grows faint. The hand places the smoker onto the ground and gently lifts the frame, densely packed with glistening, viscous honeycomb. A few bees remain, buzzing drowsily here and there; the smoke makes them think the hive is on fire, which makes them gobble up the honey and retreat to the back of the hive, which makes them sluggish and unlikely to harm the beekeeper.

SUSAN'S VOICE:
Humans have lived in relation to bees for more than 10,000 years. Art and archeology agree, recording the culling of honey and wax from the wild ones, or bees kept in woven baskets, wooden boxes, and little houses made of clay. 10,000 years: we are no more human without bees than bees are apian without humans. Our exchanges with the bees are so ancient that they extend beyond metaphor to shape the structure of our consciousness: nature, civilisation, colonisation, order, productivity, value. Honey has sweetened the tongues of all our ancestors. Wax-coated little tablets for scratching with a stylus were used to teach children to write, and for correspondence among the elites. When the message

was no longer needed, the wax tablet was wiped clean, a precursor to Freud's "Mystic Writing Pad." The 19th-century invention of wax cylinders for recording sound was a throwback to their use in the 7th century BC for tablets and amulets among the Greeks and Etruscans. Wax has fuelled our candles, sealed our stitches, polished our tools and coated our bodies.

CLOSE UP ON THE HANDLE OF A KNIFE PROTRUDING OUT OF A POT OF BOILING WATER

The gloved hand removes the knife from the pot. It's an uncapping knife for collecting beeswax, long and rounded. The hand scrapes the frame of honeycomb slowly and evenly, from top to bottom, gathering thick layers of wax. This repeats for a few hypnotic cycles until the blade cools. A few bees circle the metal bucket into which the wax has been heaped.

SUSAN'S VOICE:
There are two kinds of wax best used in sculpture:

Pure beeswax: it's yellow, when melted down, becomes clear and transparent. A medium that connects the artist to the foundations of his or her humanity: we have been domesticated by the bees for so long.

Then there is Carnauba wax, which is more expensive: opaque, shellac, light brown colour. It comes in shards or flakes, made from beating the wax out of the dried leaves of the Copernicia prunifera *palm tree native to northern Brazil. It melts at higher temperatures, becoming translucent, and when it sets it is harder than any other wax. It's used in a lot of polishes and cosmetics.*

Paul saw how Jasper used beeswax and started working with it too. Technological Reliquaries, he called these slabs of fantastic, freakish meat: human, animal, monstrous. He wanted to horrify people, he said. The cheaper the materials the better. I was collecting notes at the time to write a novel about a wax sculptor named Thomas Faulk who was in the middle of an emotional breakdown. I was trying not to be in the middle of an emotional breakdown myself. I was lovers with Jasper and confused about what I was creating with Paul. We were always creating things with our conversations, but I felt myself growing restless, distant, cold, even as he tempted me with the heat of the bodies he was sculpting.

EXT. RATNER'S DELICATESSEN, OCTOBER 1965 - NIGHT

The neon sign reading RATNER'S glows red, the storefront is brightly lit showing a packed restaurant, a staple of Lower East Side nightlife.

INT. RATNER'S DELICATESSEN, OCTOBER 1965 - NIGHT

Tables of people gesticulating wildly in conversation, laughter, camping it up together. SUSAN SONTAG and PAUL THEK are sitting at a table with two mugs of steaming coffee and empty plates strewn with a few crumbs and crumpled napkins. SUSAN is a young white women in her mid-thirties, dark hair and dark eyebrows, this is around the time she was posing for Andy Warhol's 'Test Shots'. PAUL is a young white man also in his mid-thirties, a dirty blonde with a swooping fringe, clean-shaven, this is the year Peter Hujar photographed him nude astride a stuffed zebra.

PAUL:

It's about the transubstantiation of anything! Or everything. Into body and blood, the dying bodies that labor to make all things possible, all things available; buildings, food, clothing, makeup. Usually you go into a gallery and everything is so white, so cold. We've paid a terrible price for abstract expressionism: total abstraction from what's actually happening all around us, numbness. The chilliness removes you from reality, the canapés and the fancy wine create the worst kind of artifice. Rich people are insensitive, repressed, polite, just being around them desensitizes you and all the art in the vicinity. I want to use a different kind of artifice to force you to go somewhere really specific. The horror of your own flesh. The people that are dying while you get to live.

With flesh made of wax, a physical reality confronts you no matter what: either you really see it as a body, or you see through the substrate and mystically connect with ten thousand years' worth of bodily and bloody collaborations with living creatures that can swarm and sting you to make that wax. You don't have to interpret it, you can just look: whatever you do there is no escape from feeling. Even you can't think your way out of this one, Susan. I will shove your mind back into your body so help me god!

SUSAN:
She smiles and sips her coffee.

*It's such a spiritual project—but tied to making actual objects,
harnessing consciousness to flesh.*

But they're still just scattered limbs, fragments of former life kept in cages. What is the sum of all the parts? Or is that it—they remain fragmented to make it easier for me to believe I am whole? Or in keeping with the theme of Christian relics, are they awaiting their reconstitution at some Final Judgement? And does that make you Jesus, Paul?

They both laugh.

FADE OUT

INT. WAX MUSEUM - OPENING SCENE FROM "MYSTERY OF THE WAX MUSEUM" (1933).

The black and white scene pans over wax figures in period attire. It's historic whiplash: a woman dressed in the height of 18th-century French fashion holding a handkerchief; a table of medieval monks in their robes. There are cruel pairings: wax Native Americans being held a gun point by a white soldier; to their left, figures surrounding the personification of Liberty after Eugéne Delacroix's *Liberty Leading the People* (1830); the camera rests on the hands of the sculptor IVAN IGOR as they shape wax into flesh. Cut to IGOR's face as he puffs on a cigarette in deep concentration.

SUSAN'S VOICE:

The history of waxwork is born from bloodshed, shaped by trauma. Young Marie Grosholtz, later Madame Tussaud, learned her craft as a child. She sculpted her first waxwork of the philosopher Voltaire in 1777, but perfected the art only after a near-death experience. Working as a Royal tutor, she had been sentenced to execution. In a twist of fate, she was spared and released from prison and spent the following years of terror and bloodshed obsessively sculpting models of those who had died, collateral to the Revolution. Voltaire's world had been thoroughly destroyed. The oldest surviving among her works is that of King Louis XV's mistress, t Comtesse du Barry, a holy whore who fell to the guillotine in 1793 for helping other people escape. Grosholtz's teacher Philippe Curtius had started the statue; when he died in 1794, Grosholtz completed it. One hundred and seventy years later, you can see the figure of the dead woman on display in London.

In 1795 she became Madame Tussaud, and started touring her waxworks—and those she had inherited from her dead teacher Curtius—around Europe. Settling in a permanent location in London—Baker Street, 1802, long before Sherlock Holmes set up shop—the most popular feature of the museum was known as its Chamber of Horrors: a display of the famed victims of the Revolution, including their death masks, and an array of notorious criminals. Over the course of the 19th century, the exhibition expanded to include the latest thieves and murderers of the moment. In the 20th century this attraction was tempered with the representation of historical figures, famous "freaks," and eventually, celebrities. Celebrity itself being a social construction born from sensationalised murderers and unimaginable violence. This long trajectory is densely compacted in Michael Curtiz's 1933 horror film Mystery of the Wax Museum *starring Lionel Atwill, remade as* House of Wax *in 1953 with Vincent Price, one of the first 3D movies. Arguably, modelling in wax figure depicting dramatic scenes from the past had been gesturing all along toward the invention of cinema, play with wax within film a perfect storm of visceral media messaging. In both movies, the protagonist-villain avenges the destroyed wax figures he loved as if they were human, by murdering humans and coating them in wax to depict his favourite moments in history, assimilating the present to the past in all its horrors.*

As the 4-minute scene progresses IGOR welcomes DR. RASMUSSEN and an art critic named GALATALIN into his wax museum for a tour, showing them the eerily lifelike figures of JOAN OF ARC. VOLTAIRE, and MARIE ANTOINETTE, with whom he is obsessively fixated.

The sound of dialogue from the film returns:

GALATALIN:
I never saw anything more exquisite. Tell me, where did you begin to model in wax?

IGOR:
In my native country, at first as a hobby.

RASMUSSEN:
He had a great reputation as a sculptor.

IGOR:
Oh you are very kind, sir. However I was commissioned to come to England, and at the completion of my work I turned my mind more seriously to this, because it seemed to satisfy me more. I felt I could reproduce a warmth and flesh and blood of life far more better in wax, than in cold stone.

FADE OUT

INT. A STUDIO APARTMENT, NEW YORK, 1987.

The apartment is crammed with books, papers, paintings on old newspaper and canvas alike. A notebook is open to a page of a repeated doodle: banners that read in loopy handwriting "GET OVER YOURSELF;" a purple firmament of yellow stars with the words "Afflict the comfortable, COMFORT THE AFFLICTED," another of a comet tearing across the pupil of an eye. The old, sunken sofa is made into a bed on which PAUL, looking gaunt, with longer hair and a wispy beard, reclines on. SUSAN sits on a chair next to him reading from a Rainer Marie Rilke's *Duino Elegies*:

SUSAN:
Reciting The First Elegy:
Who, if I cried out, would hear me among the Angelic Orders?

*And even if one were to suddenly
take me to its heart, I would vanish into its
stronger existence. For beauty is nothing but
the beginning of terror, that we are still able to bear,
and we revere it so, because it calmly disdains
to destroy us. Every Angel is terror.
And so I hold myself back and swallow the cry
of a darkened sobbing. Ah, who then can
we make use of? Not Angels: not men,
and the resourceful creatures see clearly
that we are not really at home
in the interpreted world.*

PAUL:
Listening, then interrupts
Rilke was against interpretation!
He Laughs weakly.

SUSAN:
Wow, yes, I suppose so. Rilke was against interpretation.

PAUL:
Against interpretation, that feels so long ago.

SUSAN:
Another lifetime. And yet because it was so tied trying to articulate what the world is like, and that hasn't changed, we're still stuck living with it.

PAUL:
Haunted by the ghost of a boring old idea.

SUSAN:
Me more than you.

PAUL:
You brought it on yourself by writing it all up!

SUSAN:
But you were working on it too, in your own way, with your meat pieces.

PAUL:
Yes but they reached their conclusion; those pieces were a death practice, an acknowledgement that I felt surrounded by death and I wanted to share that with everyone. I wanted death to connect us. It was a real hippie trip I was on. And then I wanted the idea to die so I killed it and entombed the hippie. In a giant pink triangle! I can't believe I'm saying this, but given everything that was happening with the war at the time, charred bodies projected everywhere on screens and papers in such a disturbing and intimate way, who would have thought death would come so much closer than that? Who would have thought that pink pyramid would come back to haunt me?

SUSAN:
You're a true artist, Paul, and as an artist you always were ten steps ahead of everyone else, if not leaps and bounds.

PAUL:

The world is catching up.

SUSAN:

The world is catching up.

PAUL:

But Susan, I want you to remember this when you give my eulogy: My paintings are the most important things in my life. And then you, of course.

A Pause. SUSAN looks taken aback, hold her breath, like she's holding back tears. She puts down the book and takes PAUL's hand. They sit and hold hands in silence.

Brooke Palmieri

a trip to the mainland

Things fall out of me
clean.
I'm here and you are here
and
we are all at sea.

The dark was close:
the sky and sea both.
And now less and less so.

four croissants,
all wormed askew in the oven
from
their Perfect Shape

What oven - whose?
An oven on this long boat?

*

Things fall out of me
clean, and this makes me doubt them.
I'm at sea and Thek's here.
Daylight's now come over the
interior of the buffet room. At six, first
thing, the dark outside
was close,
conspiratorial over the baked beans,
conspiratorial standing over the industrial toaster,
waiting for the drop.

The light's come over now outside
and people are generally ignoring it.
Their voices get louder
as the room fills, as
more mini croissants get

ploughed thru. My
fourth has a raised
central claw, a hook.

& I don't want to look
at another winking
eye of yours.

you are processing
processing
you metabolise everything,

you traced around your
palm in pen
like they do at school,

(That's not a way to get a hand drawn!)

You circled around your
palm in pen,
and said to Susan underneath, *I love you*
You said *I'm against
interpretation,* and she
heard and wrote it down.

*

& so here, do we
intend to interpret?
is there anything, or any
body, here today to interpret?

Of his writing – it's like
he's asking for it, asking
for a close reading by
kin,

OR, it's all just for
"the others", for them
to conspire with and walk through.
to make it a passage for their message.

A person in a t-shirt walks by on the ferry.
'Chlorine is my perfume' it says.

Paul (a chosen name) worked
towards an ecology of earth and spirit resources.
~~~~~~~~~> earth as sex and
grub and slumber,
drinking
&the spirit as those things
considered, plus everything
else.

you use the pair of words *ecumenical symbol,*

(there's no internet here so I can't check, again, what this means)

All the images are at the
point of rising up,
at the point of
breaking, as waves.

Considering utter superfluity
I read that
not all resin fossilises to become amber.

The hand and the hunky drawing of
himself as momento: he's like a
teenager, sending this to Susan.
Like a teenager too, H came on a letter and sent it across
the ocean to me.

*

I'm at sea again, only
4 nights since, and more
of the same. The line
running below the football on its tiny screen
says
McDonald's to give Prize of free food 'for life'.
I have a heineken and watch the game,
reading in the breaks and when the emergency procedure video
comes on for a second time.

We know a text is a room:
bunches time and place at once and together.
We also know it is a room you can come back to.

So, this, a room for
this difficult person,
these difficult people
at this date and time, and at this
quantity of melancholy.

Right now, any holding is a half-
holding, every pleasure
feels contained by date and time.

Earlier, as a last resort, I clicked an information
button in a station to get advice. They're not
helpful.

Leave me
trying to buy a ticket
with the words 'good luck.'

Kate Morgan

Come true dreams

of moon-chasing and finding otherwise.
This is about exits. A trance, a defenestration
met by planet traffic, star sins, a sexual pain,
a pinup with purple strokes, and light confining
my shadows to a shoe. Foot nestled in a territorial
pout. Eye like a fish with heavenly reach
eternal. You crack my jaw and know there's more
to this meat than broken telephone philosophy.
If you sit in my moan, if you arrive at autumn's
saltwater shiver, you lose your breath. A star
or flamingo flock scurries home. Here,
Catullus in the canthus of your eye where there
is only holy flame, no more chicken shit. Come,
curtsy, carry me.

Ashleigh A. Allen

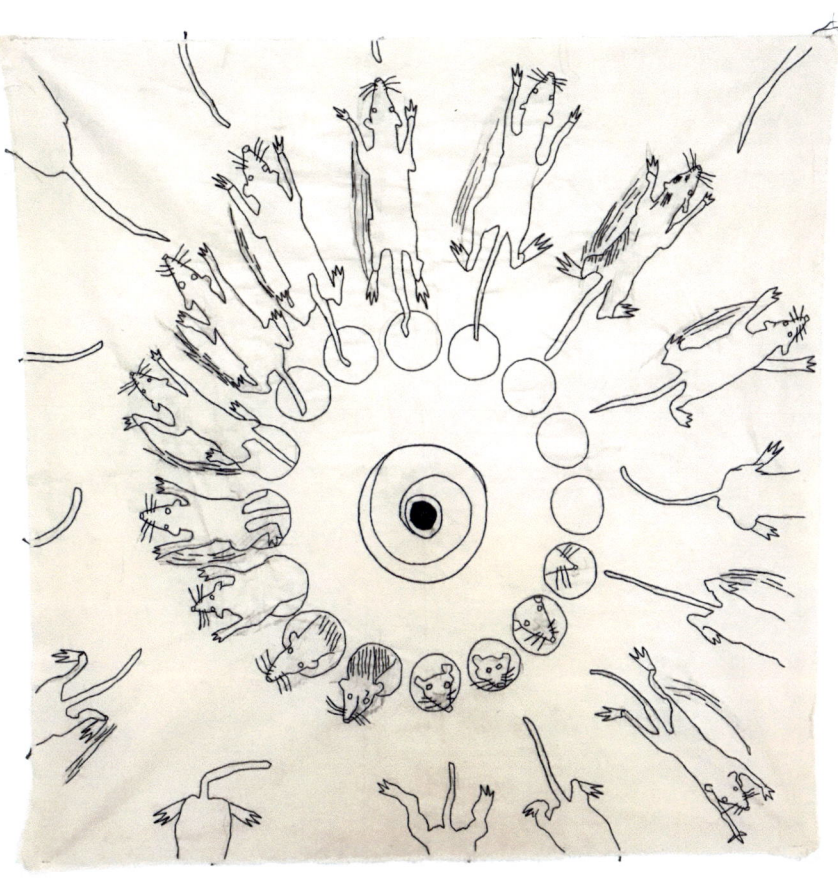

Diogo Gama

e.yet.it.led

there is a man standing in the window.
there is a man standing.
standing in the window is a man.
a man is standing.there in the window.
look.over there at the window.
at the man.
standing.
he balances on one leg.
his other in a bucket of concrete.
not concrete.but plaster.
he is making a plaster cast of his leg.
he is against interpretation.
art and all its metaphors.
it's just a leg.
a reliquary of war.
of the tomb.
of a life.cut.
short.

*eye of newt.of the beholder.of the storm.an apple.of an eagle.
black.blind.bullseye.back of one's head.back and to the left.*

the eyes of stars are scattered.
blinking out.
one by one.
all those beautiful boys.
andy's boys.
winking at the screen test.
puffing out their chests.
their cocks jutting forth.
earnestly.honestly.
their comet will not shine alone.
in wind and sun and rain.
these mangled flowers and lesser shadows.
the sky is a purple rainhaze.
the stars are brilliant specks of light.

pricking my eyes.
poking them out.

*eye of newt.of the beholder.of the storm.an apple.of an eagle.
black.blind.bullseye.back of one's head.back and to the left.*

the invisible sun stretches across the corn.
clouds race over the sea.
whose light shines on the flower of the morning.
the mourning of a world confined by colour.
the egg has entered the waters of heavens.
the egg is opening.
it bursts forth.
from its eye a yellow yolk.
doused in purple paraffin.
fly away peter.fly away paul.
standing at the gates of heaven.
standing naked.tall.
black and white.
imperial purple with threads of gold.
you will never grow old.
we give thanks and praise.
to the brave that died.in darkness.
in fear.solitude.
we wait for the wild spring.
it's coming.
the heavens have foretold it.
the shining comet reflects the stars in our eyes.
echoes.the egg.of hearts.
the wood of pines.cloven.
hooved.
smell their scent
we're coming.cometclothed.
in glory.
hallelujah.

JP Seabright

bye to your corpse

There is always something to be learnt
from meeting a corpse, is breathing. I-

orient myself at the foot of a
page - the page on its back.

The start is a sun picked fly away
hair - I kill the heart how it tells me.

1911- Watches Halley's comet pass by earth
on May 18th.
1931- Paints Self Portrait with Plucked Eye
(the subjects right).
1938 - Loses eye during a bar fight in Paris
(the subjects left).

When I think of execution, I think of the pain—
the discipline— of doing those things and how
easy it is to remain literal, symmetrical,
         -his ear- to -his chest, yes.
           But there is nothing easy about this.
               How a private heart beats-
Pry-vat-ly. And hearing yours; a sound of brushed
metal sliding against itself as we revolute
through degrees of clarity, convey image, make
apparent, make sense of -*Pukes*. Our reason is
reproduced.

    Where is the mind when not in words?

In your studio, (Incense burning here) everything is
partial, in progress - so the shadows redress
themselves casually every hour or so. A furniture
of cats moves the conversation around, but never
forwards; the politics stay uneaten. *Idea for a-*

That picture of you by the sea, I mean, arms - I'm
saying we could have been matter or a plant.

A vulture circles a ruin to indicate that meaning
propels itself- it allows these places teach -
                          glides
It moves a highlight in the big impacted
eye of an oracular kid. Close, open. Now, having
understood, action, gesture, rotation, elbow, wrist
(vein), hand (half-eaten), fingertips for flames.
              The past develops blood vessels
and we grow diseases in our blood,
but illness is a childhood, we advance pronate,
splayed in white rib and oversized hoodies-we are
seedy agents who are bad catholics on a mission
they don't believe in blissy in our arms, slow
blinking like cum-drunk cats to the white sky
while armoured white horses rear up and whinny
in the distance, clip disappear in the furnace
of memory.

1986- Watches
1987- Paints
1988- I'm saying we could have been matter or a
plant and not have had a heart to kill.

                              Hugo Hagger

I hope!

You hear it when I write your name
carved in clean line and sharp flame
and behold the sound as a sign:
a star falling cleaved your eye.
Oh, how I loved you
old love of mine.

Cowboy

I let my hunger lead the way
and I've learned
I have an appetite for dead ends
and that I feel like a man
when I chase difficult loves.
What a foolish girl I am. My father's son
there's no mistaking it.
I call out of the blue
from a pay phone
to you on earth,
leaning against a wall
with a paper cup of coffee
and my sleeves rolled up,
the sundial of my shadow
keeping a time
that no longer exists.
Don't tell the cowboys I've learned some of their secrets.
I promise –
I'll write them all down
against the clouds
if you promise
to look up.

Amanda Kraley

Cosmic Joke

You were backlit by the strongest part of dusk and I felt purely orange. You stepped forward and placed hands on my shoulders. You said, Take This All In, the comet you meant. I had just arrived and felt captivated by an object moving so fast, we seemed fixed against it. Like The Moon It's Astrological, you said and I nodded as if I knew that too. The east moving sign reflected in your pupil. It drifted to my right, coordinates that added depth to time. I thought the world was ending when the whites left your eyes. Your new name has seen more falling stars than the old one. I'm About To Change you told me. You released my shoulders and presented shimmering hands that captured eras. Strings of golden blonde hair stuck to your sweaty angular face that became something made more for sky or sea than earth. Your new form arrived at nightfall and you said A Cosmic Alignment, It's Wild Right? I said wild back to you and turned against a Palermo street wall. There, I told you I'm a time traveler without looking at your new body. Your new wings pushed your powerful frame against me. Your linens were now tattered on scaly purple skin over new muscles. I went limp into to your mythological body. I turned my head back to your electric lashes surrounding amaranthine pools, the colors of Lakers but we were never meant for California. We laughed in the face of your transition. Fangs stuck from a simple mouth that told me Let's Go Higher. You held me over the darkening city and I pressed my entirety against you. I felt closer to the spray of galactic ice that made you. We hovered over the entrance to your Venice and landed at the door of a tomb. It was as cool in the cellar of bodies as in the air. We're Two More Skulls Down Here you said. You took me deep into the archive illuminating a path of sconces with a torch. You stopped and I watched you lean against your familiar ancient beam. In the catacombs I said you were famous for not wanting me to do this. You asked me Do What? I said to read into you when I only wanted to feel. Feel It you commanded and you put my hand on your crotch. I stroked its outline, an exaggerated explorer and the last desperate fabrics fell off you to the stones. You had grown impossibly large, I stepped back as your figure blocked the wall of compartments. I told you it wasn't necessary to hide their view, that they would have kept our secret. You said This Is Just For You and stroked your satyr endowment. I got the reference and could not take it without magic. You raised hairy, clawed feet into the air and made your monstrous body an offering. I nearly disappeared within you, a fellow traveler who rode you in the subterranean. I led your tail into me and our speculative bodies became a circular track. You raised me off the floor, to a deeper connection, more light than fluid. I could have unloaded forever and you told me In The Future You'll Still Be Waiting For A Sign.

Brendan Cook

I

We made a mess in
Your Chevette way back in May
1989.
In a gravel parking lot,
Cum all over my new suit.

Thought I was hot shit
With my Depeche Mode look and
Gas money in my
pocket, New Order on the
decks and all eyes on my ass.

Our clothes strained against
The mass of us, both a threat
And a promise, hung
heavy, suspended between
Sign and signification.

"Are you gonna be
Still in love with me after
The lights go up and
The last beat has sounded?" Babe,
You don't even know my name.

The 909 rolled
And our bodies kept jumping,
Between thumps shouting,
"The cymbals! They're samples!" I
Bit my lip and kept rolling.

Rubberband basslines
Called me back to a primal,
Feral place inside
That wants to be called a soul
If the word weren't yet used up.

II

So many were sick:
Joe, that magic, gorgeous blond,
Others we didn't
Know. They were all just shadows
Graying the rays of our light.

The storied stones were
Thrown a score of years before
And a wall arose
Between those who remembered
And those who had never known.

Brash adolescence
Rode triumphant over them.
Its immunity
To all consequence is what
They most desired and envied.

With a pocket full
Of posies, a lissome boy
On a sunlit path
Neared a darker hollow where
They could not help but follow.

III

The plague, the sickness,
The creeping death. A king in
His crown. A syringe
His sceptre, a skull his orb.
For his regal cape, a quilt.

He causeth now this
Last week of February
The barren rose bush
To bloom. The dense stem trembles,
The buds burst anew, blood-bright.

A false miracle—
The blossoming will not cease.
The efflorescence
Spills forth, reddening the earth.
What once were knolls become graves.

Beneath his heel he
Snaps in half the bones of those
whom we have loved best.
Their screams are smothered by the
Thunk thunk thunk of our good times.

And the show is not
Over. It plays out even
now, on a loop, as
More characters crash into
An already crowded frame.

Born of corrupt and
cracked minds these hymnal visions—
A blond youth—a beach—
A cavern of supplicants—
Roiling up in convulsions.

In stale sickrooms lie
The careworn ruins of once
Sun-bronzed Apollos—
Cadaverous, consumptive,
Vanquished by their own bodies.

Infection arrives
enveloped, like a letter.
To its cruel message
All men must pay obeisance.
It is a royal decree.

It strangles them. False
Evidence appears real, then,
Through repetition,
Becomes real. They seek to speak
Against it but are silenced.

Officials deceive
And obfuscate. They believe
Their high position
Preserves them, but their blood will
Slake the King's thirst just the same.

IV

When did this other,
The one who looks back from the
Glass with doubting eyes,
Emerge? How did he come to
Be so frayed and depleted?

His face hangs in jowls,
The flesh pocked and lined, all of
Its late luminance
Gone dark. He will not meet my
gaze. He is old and fearful.

V

The square is empty.
The director has blocked the
scene, but the actors
Will not appear. They have gone,
Swallowed in silvery fog.

Accelerando.
The book is not on the shelf.
Thirteen hours from now
It will be forgotten or
found. Immaterial text.

Fare—Italian—
Irregular—to make, do.
Sognare—to dream.
The words, images appear,
Appall—an impasse only.

First come the numbers
And then the numbers are named.
But names become noise,
Lost in the logarithmic,
Zeroes appended to them.

Panic overflows,
The Atlantic goes silent.
The East bends aside,
The West sets itself alight,
The volcano blows tonight.

The discourse forces
Us into stocks and fetters,
Manners of speaking
That bind us to compliance,
Fancies of civility.

Liability
Is limited in love and plague.
Our corporeal
Forms dissolve, liquidate,
Cannot be called to account.

The canals run clear!
Dolphins play in the harbor!
The quarantined sing
Above them! From death,
Lies will rise if we let them.

VI

In imperfect mouths
Exhalations smoothed, rounded
Like the pebbles at
Nickel Plate Beach just where our
Shallow bay licks at the shore.

A thin envelope
Holds your obituary.
If I keep it sealed—
Preposterous already—
These thoughts will not bear thinking.

Matt Bailey

Heat from this Contagious Sun

'... the world was falling apart, anyone could see it...'.
Paul Thek, 1981

In 1619 Gotthard Arthusius, a German historian, published a lavishly illustrated pamphlet after sighting a Great Comet. He announced that 'we have seen such a sign in our time for Almighty God has put a cruel torch in the sky and shown us a Comet with a very long and burning tail'. Arthusius proceeded to list the disasters that accompanied comets, warning of earthquakes, floods, war, treason and epidemics.

In 1864, English poet Gerard Manley Hopkins wrote an ominous fragment of poetry in his diary:

I am like a slip of comet…
I have drawn heat from this contagious sun:
To not ungentle death now forth I run

In 1985, American artist Paul Thek painted a flashing comet reflected in someone's eye, using purple and yellow acrylic on canvas board. Thek's comet too could symbolise a terrifying contagion, the HIV epidemic that has ravaged the world. The painting was discovered in his storage following his death from AIDS in 1988.

A cosmic *memento mori*, the comet streaks through the imagination of these three men, bringing with it fear of disaster, epidemic, death. The comet has a long history of petrifying humanity. Throughout recorded history they have been seen as bad omens: 'bearded stars' which signal the end of days. Rooted in Christian beliefs, the years 1200 to 1650 signalled peak 'comet fear', a deep felt terror that the comet heralded an apocalypse.

In 1963, Thek visited the Capuchin catacombs of Palermo with his friend and lover, Peter Hujar. There Hujar photographed him standing nonchalantly in front of the mummified bodies. Thek recalled that 'it delighted me that bodies could be used to decorate a room like flowers'. Life and death became both subject matter and medium.

Raised in a Catholic family, the sacred and the profane tussled within his practice, and Thek was driven by the conflicting forces of art, sexuality and religion. Fascinated with funerals and cycles of life, he wrote in a notebook that 'my work is about time, an inevitable impurity from which we all suffer'.

Does this comet foreshadow the end of time? A catastrophic termination? AIDS? An American apocalypse? Ronald Reagan's piss poor response to the 'gay plague'? The end of Thek's own life?

In 1985, Thek produced another painting using the same startling purple and yellow. Titled *Afflict the Comfortable, Comfort the Afflicted*, rather than showing a single comet – the words seem to be floating in a sea of stars.

The pair can be viewed as companion pieces – a call to arms to disrupt security, to cause havoc, to practice radical tenderness, to begin afresh. Thek had 'understood that a new unity had to be created' and sought to '[anchor the] self in a more encompassing context ... God, nature, life and death, symbol'.

Rather than an end, maybe Thek's comet signals a beginning. The abolition of one system to make space for another – a place where queer people can be celebrated rather than vilified, and togetherness rules the world.

Charlotte Flint

Cosmology

Plato asserts in his Cosmology that every soul
has a companion star to which it returns upon death.

Alone in the darkness
I lie on the lawn.
Looking up at the night sky
I search for you.
A few lonely stars
look down at me.
They yearn in vain
for Cassiopeia, for Copernicus,
for Ganymede and you.
A comet streaks across the sky,
across my eye.
Now I have found you.

Rodney Schreiner

Far from an eye; indifferent, absorbed, endless.
Moving then, or remaining still, shored in a luminous halo—for an eye.
An eye that falls and flys, inaudible.
A mythical, magical relic—of an eye.
Innocence: mooned, the stars: sad and lovely, yet bleeding.
Holy and golden, but now falling: cruel, onto loves glowing g-olden days dust.
Bittersweet love[s], still remaining.

Lucy Price

Gutter

I remember the day the blazing star
fell and we knew we were fucked -
its dazzling comet-tail caught my eye
dragged across the sky painted
with constellations and planes soaring.
I was flooded with foreboding, gutted.

You had just pulled out of my guts
hand still warm on my shoulder, a star
-crossed casual encounter. I'm sore,
a burning falling angel grasping at a fuck
to tether me to the frozen universe. Painted
insides already cold, you can't meet my eye.

Later fear and desperation whispers I'm
careful, clean, not like them - the lies I utter
on my knees, smelling of turps and paint
prayer caught in my mouth. He's hard, I'm starved
and choking, begging, revelling in connection. Fuck
me raw, fuck me harder, faster, deeper, 'till I soar.

Afterwards I shower scrub and scour pink sores
in blistering heat, scold my scarred self but both I
and the fogged up mirror know this fuckup
will recur. Like Oscar I never could resist gutters
and temptation, trade and tricks, seeking starlight
above, dizzying sparkles in my eyes. I should paint

portraits of pretty boys, lovers mourned, paint
each Icarus before he burns up, ash soaring
skyward - but sight is sketchy. This cursed star
marks every horoscope a bad moon rising. I
seep lost colour, mind-muddied, a gut
-wrench roar on weeping scabby lips. Fuck!

I used to cry fuck me blind, now fuck
me full of fire, make me vital. I'll paint
one last self portrait - a guttering,
waxen man on the wane, bedsores
bedridden, plagued by wheezing. I'm
a study in pain and hope so stark.

Close up on my fucked body - a canvas eyesore
of paint-blind lesions, blood bruises. I
rise from the gutter, still fixed on stars.

Morgan Melhuish

Jordan Weitzman

Untitled (island with meteor)

We're on the island. We're outdoors. It's night. I see several meteors in the sky. In short succession the meteors pass. They don't burn across the sky: they appear briefly, moving from point A to a nearby point B before disappearing.

The island is an old fortress. All these interconnected islands are full of 18th century military architecture. We came to the island to party. We're a twenty minute ferry ride and a ten minute walk away from the center of Helsinki. The distance from land means less light pollution in the sky. It makes watching the meteors easier.

We're standing outside. The party is indoors. People from the art world dance in a circle. Their moves are tentative.

A couple of hundred meters from where we are standing is a cell. In the Mid-19th century a local serial killer was tortured to death there. He was chained to the back wall of the cell, slowly dying over a year and a half. People from the city, anyone who wanted to, would come to the island and look at him. What they saw was supposed to educate them.

I only come to the island for the events, or to go swimming. It takes effort to remember what I know about the people who met their violent deaths here. These deaths don't feel relevant to the night. I place a cigarette between my lips and inhale.

You know better. You know why the meteors are here, I mean there, in sight, at the end of our atmosphere. You tell me it's the time of the Perseids. The best, most plentiful meteor showers of the year, the Perseids occur on warm summer nights, you read to me from your phone.

In Finnish, the word 'perse' means ass. It's a crude and forward expression. The presence of 'perse' within the Perseids makes an otherwise poetic word vibrate in a dumb way. The Finnish language reliably brings down any grand, romantic notion. It's not unlike gravity.

Look, another meteor! You turn your head. You've missed it.

What is depicted in Thek's painting is, I guess, not a meteor. Meteors are space rocks that burn up in the earth's atmosphere, you read to me from your phone. Comets are icy dirtballs that orbit the sun, you read. I could have known that. I spent too many years in school daydreaming, drawing, looking out of the window and hating myself. I've let knowledge pass me by.

In Thek's painting one sees a very small comet and a very large eye. The majority of the painted surface is made up of a purple earth or body of water, a 'background' out of which the outline of the eye rises. I could see it as a sketch for a grand piece of land art, a kind of spiral jetty, something you'd witness from above, from a helicopter or a space station. Maybe the comet orbits the giant eye. Maybe the comet is falling into the eye.

An eye, like a planet, is really an orb. You grasp its true dimensions when it has been removed from its socket. But the eye in Thek's painting is flat, embedded into a surface: the face of a painting.

I'm looking at an image of Thek's artwork on the screen of your phone. I don't know where the actual painting is. Thek died three years after finishing this painting, you say, and I'm trying not to make an image of his suffering. I don't want to learn anything.

The screen glows in the night. I start thinking about a poem. It's this poem from 1956, by Eeva-Liisa Manner. The language is too sophisticated, I can't translate the poem. In the poem Manner writes about swimming on God's surface, on the surface of God's cold, disinterested eyes. Eyes that see without attachment and permit everything.

I think about it a lot. Someone swimming in the eye of God like it's a cold salt water pool. I think of the frozen comet sinking into the purple depths of the eye Thek painted. The screen of your phone goes dark. I face the sky, hoping to see more meteors fall.

Jaakko Pallasvuo

> "The world to an end shall come,
> In nineteen hundred and eighty-one"

Mother Shipton, born Ursula Southell outside of Knaresborough, Yorkshire in 1488, was a soothsayer known for predicting historical events, including the End of Days. She was born to a teenage mother during a thunderstorm in a cave by the River Nidd, where nearby stood (and stands today), a dropping well. It is called this because the sulfate content in its waters calcifies objects and hangs them in stony suspension. This association led to the idea that Shipton "petrified" those who crossed her, like a Medusa. Today, the cave and the well are considered England's oldest tourist attraction.

In 1980, Walter Alvarez proposed the theory that the extinction of the dinosaurs was caused by an "extraterrestrial projectile" crashing to Earth, creating a "kill mechanism." Waves drowned and earthquakes rocked the land, sulfate dust poisoned the air and blocked out the sun, cooling the earth and freezing the plants and soon, the animals. Dinosaurs stand frozen still, bones reassembled behind velvet ropes in museums, or as sculptures arranged interacting like those in Crystal Palace Park in London.

Mark Twain, born Samuel Langhorne Clemens in Florida, Missouri in 1835, was an American author who predicted his own death as being in proximity to the arrival of Halley's Comet, which had also ushered in his birth seventy-five years before.

"The Almighty has said, no doubt, "Now here are these unaccountable freaks; they came in together, they must go out together."

Alex Fiorentino

Will-o'-the-wisp
(four perspectives)

Someone called me *sun-blindness*. Said I was that burning, temporary affliction; pain and light at once. Someone called me *sun-blindness*, because I made them momentarily lose their ability to see and perceive and judge. I made them lose their way and they liked it. (You're going to lose your way and like it.) Someone called me *sun-blindness* because they wanted to see me and couldn't. (It's not something you really see after all. Brief and dazzling, you feel its effect, feel it visually, in the eye. You're blinded as it moves through you. I move through you and blind you.)
/
I like cropping up. Materialising from the mist on the road.
I like stepping into the path of someone's fast-moving life.
/
You've seen me before now. I know we've only just met, but you have seen me before. You were walking in some distant place, a forest, thick. Deep in there waited a premonition, a vision, a version of me. A sudden clearing, something in the sky. The incongruity pierced you, blinded you, made you turn and move away quickly so that thin, barbed twigs were stuck to your hood by the time you made it back to the path.
/
I think occasionally about that man. The sad one who was visiting from abroad. The one who slipped me a fifty in the park for nothing. For just being there with him. Said *see you later, okay?* The *okay* was what did it. The hook of it. The way he tried to hook me with that word. It repelled me. I smiled at him, looked him in the eye so that he'd think I was being sincere. I nodded with that calm, open smile before turning away, knowing his *later* wouldn't be the same as mine.

Harald Smart

dramatis personae blatta[1]

sometimes, hope is the opposite of history
and history comes and has already

re-member scenes played out in rooms
from before the cafes where they smoked
real smokes and toasted drinks
that could really fuck you up

~

back then, in plum, bruise, sarcoma blues
before the music stopped and the lights came up
and the one you liked went home with someone else
and then someone said they were in love
and then someone said they were gone

and you could be historical about the body but
you would be missing
           some other
                        context

~

a dream can be a whole future
inconvenient dust on convenient griefs
comes in blue and stays in white streaks

and that's how history makes
a whole body out of body
parts that look so much like your own
body parts you can't stand to
look at them

---

[1] purple, cockroach, moth, beetle (latin)

~

why so delft blue and where to travelling?
re-member, mottled rock, skin, a mouth
re-member, that old toy
forgotten-because-kitsch on the back seat long after
friends who shared coffee and gossip and smokes

and a star holds its own light
but is always also a memory of light
more in the dominion of moons, really

~

the eye holds it like hope or stage lights or a single tear
all glinting back some old fervent moment

obscured by life, dust can be beautiful, too,
when viewed through ice crystal blue: the past
is a lens we learn to hold right,
to train upon the end as an object that dreams
the catastrophic disintegration of the final fourth wall
the word: over.
we know, we know, we know.

loll jung

Untitled

Fantasy is the negation of the negation of the world.

At the edge we fall off, over a wave and away, through the blue, that becomes simultaneously not a blue, that becomes unnamable, that is so bright the eyes are burned and so dark one may never see again.

Once upon a time in the eye of the beholder, a world unfolded in the deep lapis, in the folds of a heavy cloth edged in gold, its woven riches spilling forth.

There is no through there is only around, deep depth of cloud steeped in darkness, the sky is all encompassing, the heavens open.

Channels of air, that becon of sound.
The voice of a space, of all space, reedy and swelling in haunting creshendo, thin and long.

Into the imagined space of the more than, in the pinprick of apeture and gaping mouth of the chasm.
In times of ritualistic meaning the membranes between us grow thin, we hang in gauze like layers and space between, our many parts.

Learned rhythms spill forth, an immersion, of all around.

To make that soul a star that burns forever.[1]

All seeing, weeping as it encompasses, consuming, holding forth.
Crying. Flung.

Floats, soars, majestically; a doomed flight,
or an ever expiring trajectory.

Ponderous, planetary. A lyric to the end.

< The scene >
of the world burning,
 collapsing around them,
arcadia falling,
the neo-classical facades crumbling.
The scale perturbed and the sun too big,
throbbing and dying in the sky.
Ash falling,
the heat of the brewing end storm,
building to the ultimate catharsis.

The framing of the good and the evil is muddied,
the seduction of beauty and of ease.

There is a dust that falls from the moth's wings as the pin passes through the resin, as the clear substance drowns them, as they fulfil their position. They become a gridded collection. This dust lets them fly, or lets their wings work, this dust is a part of their body, their being, even as it is unattached. It falls gently when they are handled, caught, trapped. Except that a gentle shower of dust is a violent shedding, a wounding, tantamount to killing.
There are moths in the institutions collection with holes in their wings. Shot through, a firearm, a round.

I will call it the *ungazed upon.*

---

[1] *Ovid, Metamorphosis.*

Marguerite Carson

Untitled (dream recounted for Timothy)

I'm on a plane and no one knows that I'm up here in a vacant jumbo jet with rows of economy class seating and it's dark outside but looks like some kind of stage set with cardboard clouds and stars made out of tin foil yet I'm aware of a certain height and descending over some kind of black or deep blue tarpaulin that to the naked eye seems close and secured by perhaps a concrete floor but only I know about and am obsessed by the foreknowledge that beneath the tarpaulin is nothing and in fact the sky is beneath it and this simulation is in fact an illusion of a simulation over which I am in a real plane flying in a real sky or maybe I am just suspended but I can't take my seatbelt off and I'm in the middle of the third row Seat 52 E towards the rear of the plane and despite this fixity I have full knowledge of the emptiness of this 323 seat airliner and that there is no-one in the cockpit flying the aircraft because maybe everyone vanished or maybe this is a simulation designed to scare me and maybe I have been drugged into being here and then the thought occurs to me that I am in the middle of some heist movie and the bad guys have tied me to the seat and remote-controlled the plane to steer me out over the sea and detonate a bomb loaded in the cargo hold but someone forgot to write the script and so the plane is just flying and very soon it will run out of fuel and I can either pretend to be in a heist movie or accept the illusion or the illusion of the illusion so I try turning my head toward the window and stare at the black tarpaulin below and feel the weight of my body and hard cock in the seat so as to prevent the anticipatory experience of freefall

Richard Porter

Nicholas Kalinoski

Indolent in the sun, in Key West without you, I am reminded of all the places we kept returning to, the same resorts you had gone to in the past, before we met. Waikiki in Hawaii, and the Zona Rosa in Puerto Vallarta were the main ones. You favored staying in gay hotels, in the sort of places that would be advertised in the back pages of the *Advocate,* or in the old gay travel guide *Spartacus.* "Here we can be ourselves," you'd explain. I wasn't sure what that meant. I found them uncomfortable at first. I felt judged for our age gap in a way that was more hurtful than in the straight world, where I stopped caring what others thought after I moved to the States. Yet, once I let my guard down, I would gradually warm up to the experience. During the convivial low-key communal breakfasts, I would enjoy meeting gay people from other parts of the country, listening to them describe the texture of their lives outside of major cities, hearing them explain why they'd stayed in small towns in the Midwest, and their pride in the bittersweet victory over the inevitability of exile. In the afternoon, safely hiding behind a book—Denton Welsh's *In Youth Is Pleasure,* Proust's *Swann's Way,* and Jane Bowles's *Two Serious Ladies* come to mind—I'd find the charged cruising vibe at the gay beach thrilling and anxiety-provoking in equal measure. And at night it would be comforting to run into the same guests in the endless circuit of bars and clubs.

In the mid-90s, while in Costa Rica's Manuel Antonio Bay, walking back from a swim, you hallucinated from a distance that I was your partner who had died of AIDS the year before we met. I can still access the sense of dread descending on the idyllic crescent-shaped bay, but I am not sure what to ascribe it to. Is it something that I register from your expression, as if you've just seen a ghost? Am I faced with the realization that our romance rests on a case of mistaken identity?

What was the nature of the transaction? I have the sensation of having come too late, after it mattered, after you had already experienced the defining relationship of your life. Earlier in our romance, a leader from the spiritual movement, the Brahma Kumaris, who had been trying to recruit you for years, noted my uncanny physical resemblance to your dead lover, implying a sense of supernatural intervention at play—a summoning of my presence to ease your grief. The three of us were sitting at the kitchen roundtable. Your partner had designed the whole house with such care, every piece of furniture rounded, softened, preventing you from bumping into sharp angles, which you were prone to doing. I remained silent, intimidated by the aura of self-importance that lingered around the guru, accented by the white sari she wore. I vaguely resented the implication that my sense of self, uncertain and insubstantial, would now be predicated on someone I would never meet. A Gothic mystery unveiled on a bright Saturday morning in Mar Vista, California. Around that time you gave me his gold crucifix necklace, the only thing his homophobic parents didn't take after his funeral. I accepted the offering reluctantly, maybe out of superstition. It's still tucked in my wallet, its thin chain tangled in knots. One of my art teachers says my relationship with culture is too fraught with desire and identification.

I am listening to the Pet Shop Boys' "Being Boring." I visit a website entirely dedicated to the song, and get lost in the trivia. I watch Bruce Weber's black-and-white video, shot in two days in a rental house in Long Island. The opening shot features rapid-fire edits of a naked male model from behind, first jumping on a trampoline, and later diving into a pool. Framed against a cloudy sky, the scene looks like an outtake from Leni Riefenstahl's *Olympia*. I am surprised to find out that these shots alone were enough to ban the video from being shown on MTV. All the scenes that follow showing couples making out are strictly heterosexual pairings, save from one quick edit featuring two boys sleeping in a king-size bed, a girl safely propped between them, which could, according to the viewer's taste, disrupt or enhance the homoeroticism. There's a lot of obsessive scrubbing and grooming of these antiseptic and healthy bodies, as they prepare for the party to come. There's so much foam recurring throughout, in the bathroom scenes, that you'd think this was a bubble-bath commercial. A tableau composed of a neoclassical marble bust next to a vase filled with white roses, a shot with a small white horse being led through a corridor, and a girl kissing a dove pay a light homage to Cocteau's brand of surrealism. A monkey on a tricycle circling around the crowd adds an exotic flair, and the presence of a young boy in a tuxedo makes the whole affair safe and innocent. Later at the party, a perfectly groomed white poodle yawns, maybe mirroring the audience's only possible response to the tepid spectacle.

I owned a copy of Weber's book *Rio*, which I had bought in an art gallery on my first trip to London in the late '80s. It was expensive and I felt really uncomfortable entering the uninviting white space, a double transgression. I liked the way some of the photos were tinted with purple and yellow. I was closeted and when I showed the book to a straight friend who aspired to be a photographer, he was bothered by the homoeroticism of some of the images. I tried to argue that they were not homoerotic, even though I clearly understood that they could only be perceived that way. Still the photographs possessed a kind of opacity that neutralized any projection of affects from the viewer. For all their idealized youth and beauty, the models exude what writer Rosemary Carroll qualified in a 1985 *BOMB* conversation with Weber as "a blankness and a banality that borders on cruelty." Maybe this was the perfect book at the peak of the AIDS epidemic. Was my fascination with the book a small attempt to bridge things I knew—beach culture, third-world poverty (made picturesque here), sublimated friendships—and the things I secretly desired and wouldn't admit to myself, things outside the frame, which could only be permitted in faraway resorts, in black and white, among beautiful people? We saw the Pet Shop Boys in concert during the LGBT Millennium March on Washington in 2000. You had gone to the one in 1993, where you stood by the quilt of your dead lover. You thought that seeing so many of us in one place would give me a sense of belonging to the community, and anchor my identity inside the larger political movement for our rights. In the late '70s, you took part in a two week-end, EST-inspired seminar named the Advocate Experience, which was an offshoot of the magazine and created by its editor, David Goodstein, with the help of an EST-trained therapist, Rob Eichberg. Being around a hundred gay and lesbian people, sharing traumas and confessions, rewarded by automatic applauses, had been a cathartic experience, which you credited as the turning point in your self-acceptance journey.

It was the first march since the triple-therapy regimen had brought people back from the brink of death, and there was a renewed sense of hope and purpose. After Melissa Etheridge turned the crowd wild with a paroxistic rendition of "Come through My Window," the Pet Shop Boy took the stage. It was a short set and they played "Being Boring" as the second of five songs. I'd heard it dozens of times before but only at that moment its meaning was revealed to me. It was like a wave of communal grief crashing upon the audience. The sadness and the surprise of being the one who survives, told so transparently in the third verse, bought me to tears. "Now I sit with different faces / in rented rooms and foreign places. All the people I was kissing, some are here and some are missing in the nineteen-nineties. I never dreamt that I would get to be / The creature that I always meant to be / But I thought in spite of dreams / You'd be sitting somewhere here with me." Neil Tennant describes the song as "an autobiographical elegy for my best friend from Newcastle whom I'd known since we were teenagers; he died in 1989 aged only thirty-four. [...] In the third verse I am a Pet Shop Boy recording in Munich, while back in London my friend has died and other friends are ill."

Later that night in front of the stage I ran into a straight guy I knew from our social circle in LA, Coley. I was surprised to see him there, and he explained that he'd been hired to document on video the speaking tour of Ellen DeGeneres and Anne Heche, the Lesbian power couple of the moment. He invited us to hang out backstage after the show but you wanted to hit the bars, all of them extremely crowded and festive. There I felt alienated, and undesirable, unable to start any conversations, watching you being gregarious and flirtatious from a distance, accruing a feeling of resentment. On the flight back, you asked me how the experience made me feel, if I had been transformed by the sight of a million LGBT people, and I responded something like, "I hate the LGBT community, they're all stupid. I don't want to belong to it." I watched your face turning red with anger. You didn't reply and remained silent for a long while. I felt really bad, knowing I pushed you too far, and apologized profusely. You forgave me.

We saw these resorts closing one after another, having outlived their purpose. These places became a casualty of the newfound visibility and acceptance of the gay community. I could see how that loss affected you. How it made you nostalgic for a more separatist time. On our last trip to Hawaii, the hotel in Waikiki had become a condo rental.

They had not informed you that the ownership had changed. We were now sharing our communal space with middle-class heterosexual couples with kids. One of the main bars, with an outdoor patio, had closed. And the other bar, near the hotel, had built glass structures to enclose it and smoking was prohibited. Puerto Vallarta stayed the same, the Zona Rosa still teeming with hustlers, lawlessness, a louche energy that can be found in third world country not unlike the one I'm from. But now that you're gone, we'll never experience them again, our cat-and-mouse games in foreign cities, losing and finding each other late into the night, rituals of abandonment. Walking in a delimited territory of bars, sex clubs, taco stands—our playground. And at gay restaurants, feeling the same familiar contempt from the gay waiters, the same I'd experienced since the beginning of our relationship. My life versus their life. Near exchangeability. Slow-fading currency at the southernmost point.

Hedi El Kholti

You Remain Untitled, 1985.

You left me your body entombed as art
bronze flesh that I tasted sculpted and cast

a reliquary and a lifemask
as if you knew I would need a shrine

as if my photographs were not enough
to help you escape death and the past

always present, you are not forgotten
my Paul, art passed from father to son

hung in gallery walls, sought after in books
or shared across the web, caught like dew

on a crisp morning, that glistens across
the rising City parks, our familiar grass

your art inspires, it moves,
you move me Paul, my muse

your soft moustache and straw-coloured hair
tucked behind ears on windswept beaches

gull white of your eyes, electric and alive
the milk of paradise that fed my dreams

I think of you with longing and awe
a death before death, achieved by few

resurrected with every voyeur
of your honest intellect, your artistry

those purpled sunken veins,
a blood, like paint, that slowly corrodes

the sun making a halo of your hospital head
I watched the life go out from your eyes

a single tear escapes its wax form, a candle drip
and goodbye kiss as we watch the same comet

trace its unique path across the New York sky
if only for a moment, we behold the brilliance

the infinite sublime, as the nurse closes your eyes.

Edmund Francis English

'The art works in Paul Thek's storage were inventoried after his death in 1988. There were virtually no records or reference documents of any kind. Aside from titles written on the work or published during his lifetime, works were designated as *Untitled* and descriptive titles were assigned. While working on the *Diver* catalogue with the Whitney Museum, an editorial decision was made to italicize the word *Untitled* and follow it with the descriptive title in regular type.'

Ted Bonin

Contributors

In order of appearance

E.R. De Siqueira
Ben Estes
João Motta Guedes
Lucy Swan
Jon Rainford
Louis Shankar
Amy Evans Bauer
Hattie Morrison
Sammy Paloma
AN Grace
James Horton
Nick Wood
Sophie Paul
Jae Vail
Elizabeth Zvonar
Lars Meijer
Clay AD
Michel Kessler
Pablo Miguel Martínez
Emma Harris
Dylan McNulty-Holmes
Kitya Mark
Katherine Franco
Ainslie Templeton
Alistair McCartney
John Brooks
Jesse Howarth
jimmy cooper
Felix Pilgrim
Nicholas Chittenden Morgan
Murphy O'Neir
Rachel Cattle
Isabel Nolan
Susan Finlay
Ted Simonds
Brooke Palmieri
Kate Morgan
Ashleigh A. Allen
Diogo Gama
JP Seabright
Hugo Hagger
Amanda Kraley
Brendan Cook
Matt Bailey
Charlotte Flint
Rodney Schreiner
Lucy Price
Morgan Melhuish
Jordan Weitzman
Jaakko Pallasvuo
Alex Fiorentino
Harald Smart
loll jung
Marguerite Carson
Richard Porter
Nicholas Kalinoski
Hedi El Kholti
Edmund Francis English
Ted Bonin

Responses to Untitled (eye with comet) (c.1985) by Paul Thek

Assembled by Richard Porter

Published in the U.K. by Pilot Press

978-1-7397029-3-9

All rights reserved

Printed on 100% recycled paper